HISTORY IN DEPTH

NORTHERN IRELAND 1920-82

John D. Clare

MACMILLAN

© John D. Clare 1989

All rights reserved. No reproduction, copy or transmission of this publication may be made without written permission.

No paragraph of this publication may be reproduced, copied or transmitted save with written permission or in accordance with the provisions of the Copyright Act 1956 (as amended), or under the terms of any licence permitting limited copying issued by the Copyright Licensing Agency, 33–4 Alfred Place, London WC1E 7DP.

Any person who does any unauthorised act in relation to this publication may be liable to criminal prosecution and civil claims for damages.

First published 1989

Published by
MACMILLAN EDUCATION LTD
Houndmills, Basingstoke, Hampshire RG21 2XS
and London
Companies and representatives
throughout the world

Printed in Hong Kong

British Library Cataloguing in Publication Data
Clare, John D.
 Northern Ireland 1920–1982. —— (History in depth).
 1. Northern Ireland, 1900–
 I. Title   II. Series
 941.6082
ISBN 0–333–46357–9

CONTENTS

	Preface	4
	Introduction	5
1	Northern Ireland	6
2	The Protestants	18
3	Reform	28
4	Violence	36
5	The Catholics	47
6	In search of an answer	56
	Index	72

Acknowledgements

The author and publishers wish to thank the following who have kindly given permission for the use of copyright material:

Belfast Telegraph for an extract from their 30.8.72 issue; Central Independent Television for an extract from the programme 'Too Long a Sacrifice', 1983; Seamus Deane for an extract from 'Derry', from *Gradual Wars*, Irish University Press, 1974; *Irish Times* for extracts from their 27.1.75 and 7.7.75 issues; *The Sunday Press* for an extract from their 15.8.71 issue; Times Newspapers Ltd. for material from *The Sunday Times*, 8.3.81, © Times Newspapers Ltd. 1981, and *The Times* for various extracts, © Times Newspapers Ltd.

The author and publishers wish to acknowledge, with thanks, the following photographic sources:
An Phoblacht/Republican News pp51, 64 top; Associated Press p70; Camera Press pp5, 13, 16, 18, 25, 30, 31 top, 37 bottom, 41, 46 left, 46 right, 50, 52, 54 top, 55, 59 top left, 59 top right, 59 centre; London Express News and Feature Services p67; Photo Source pp20 bottom, 26, 27 top left, 27 top right, 33, 34, 57; Popperfoto pp20 top, 23, 27 bottom, 29, 31 bottom, 35, 37 top, 40, 43, 48 top left, 48 top right, 48 bottom left, 48 bottom right, 56, 58, 59 bottom, 63, 64 bottom, 65, 66.

The publishers have made every effort to trace the copyright holders, but if any have been inadvertently overlooked, they will be pleased to make the necessary arrangements at the first opportunity.

PREFACE

The study of history is exciting, whether in a good story well told, a mystery solved by the judicious unravelling of clues, or a study of the men, women and children whose fears and ambitions, successes and tragedies make up the collective memory of mankind.

This series aims to reveal this excitement to pupils through a set of topic books on important historical subjects from the Middle Ages to the present day. Each book contains four main elements: a narrative and descriptive text, lively and relevant illustrations, extracts of contemporary evidence, and questions for further thought and work. Involvement in these elements should provide an adventure which will bring the past to life in the imagination of the pupil.

Each book is also designed to develop the knowledge, skills and concepts so essential to a pupil's growth. It provides a wide, varying introduction to the evidence available on each topic. In handling this evidence, pupils will increase their understanding of basic historical concepts such as causation and change, as well as of more advanced ideas such as revolution and democracy. In addition, their use of basic study skills will be complemented by more sophisticated historical skills such as the detection of bias and the formulation of opinion.

The intended audience for the series is pupils of eleven to sixteen years; it is expected that the earlier topics will be introduced in the first three years of secondary school, while the nineteenth and twentieth century topics are directed towards first examinations.

INTRODUCTION

A three-sided problem

In 1171–2 King Henry II of England invaded Ireland. Since then, some of the greatest names in English history have put their minds to Ireland's problems without success. Irish history is a list of failed reforms, failed repressions and failed rebellions.

Two opposing groups create the 'Irish problem'. The Unionists, most of whom are Protestants, have always wanted to be part of the United Kingdom. The Nationalists, most of whom are Catholics, have always wanted independence from England. Catholics make up about 75 per cent of the total population of Ireland. The political party Sinn Fein was formed in 1905 to campaign for independence. The problem is complicated by the involvement of the British government, which has been unable, over many centuries, to provide a workable solution.

After 1915, the Nationalists took steps to gain their independence. In 1916 the Easter Rebellion took place. In the 1918 general election, Sinn Fein gained most of the seats, set up a breakaway parliament in Dublin (the Dail Eireann), and declared independence. The Irish Republican Army (IRA) waged a fierce guerilla war. On 6 December 1921 the British government was forced to sign a peace treaty which recognised the 26 southern counties as the Irish Free State (or Eire).

Note
As you read this book, you will come across many people and organisations whose names and aims are difficult to remember. You will find a check-list in Appendix I, on page 68.

Right: *some of the unsuccessful 1916 rebels surrendering. Can you see the white 'X' which marks Eamonn de Valera, the future Prime Minister of Eire?*

Below: *Northern and Southern Ireland, 1921*

1 NORTHERN IRELAND

A bloody beginning

Most of the support for Sinn Fein in 1918–21 had come from the south of Ireland. Things were different in Ulster (the northern part of Ireland).

Half of the 50 local councils in the north wanted to join the Free State. They flew the Republican tricolour flag, and pledged their allegiance to Dail Eireann. At the same time the IRA attacked tax offices and police barracks. In June 1920 the IRA even tried to occupy the Catholic 'Bogside' area of Londonderry, but was driven out by British troops.

Most of the people who lived in Ulster, however, were Protestants. They were Unionists (sometimes called Loyalists). In 1912 many of them had signed the 'Covenant', promising to defend their 'cherished position...in the United Kingdom'. In 1920 the first Unionist leader, Sir Edward Carson, declared: 'We in Ulster will tolerate no Sinn Fein – no Sinn Fein organisation, no Sinn Fein methods.'

Edward Carson makes his point at an anti-Home Rule rally, 1913

When a policeman – District Police Inspector Swanzy – was killed by the IRA in August 1920, Loyalist mobs attacked Catholics, driving them out of their homes and their jobs. One English newspaper accused the Protestants of conducting a pogrom – an organised persecution – against the Catholics.

Sir James Craig, who had become the Unionist leader, was unmoved. He persuaded the British government to give weapons to Loyalists and by the summer of 1922 several forces of Special Constables had been set up. One Protestant in five had the legal right to hold a gun:

	Numbers	How employed	Armed?
A-Specials	5 500	Full-time, paid	Armed
B-Specials	19 000	Part-time, paid	Armed
C-Specials	?	For emergencies, unpaid	Armed
CI-Specials	7 500	Part-time, paid	Military

The Specials played an important part in resisting the IRA in Ulster, but they were untrained and on occasions attacked law-abiding Catholics. On Bloody Sunday, 10 July 1921, gangs of Specials rampaged through the Catholic areas of Belfast, killing 10 Catholics and burning 161 Catholic homes.

Using the evidence: 'The people here will defend themselves'

A   A Protestant leader visits a Catholic area after a raid:

> *[I went] up to Lisburn to see the state it was. It reminded me of a French town after it had been bombarded by the Germans as I saw it in 1916.... I found a small pair of manicure scissors that had been through the fire. I kept them as a souvenir of the event. [I heard of] some very hard cases of where Unionists had lost practically all they had by the fire of the house of a Catholic spreading to theirs.... But when one thinks of the brutal cold-blooded murder of Inspector Swanzie [sic] one does not wonder at the mob loosing [sic] its head with fury....*
>
> F. Crawford in his *Diary*, 1920

B   Memo from District Inspector Spears to the Minister of Home Affairs, 1923:

> *[A group called the Ulster Protestant Association contains] the Protestant hooligan element...whole aim and object was simply the extermination of Catholics by any and every means...met murder with murder and adopted in many respects the tactics of the rebel gunmen...deliberate and cold-blooded murder of harmless Catholics...shooting into Catholic houses and areas and throwing bombs into the houses of Catholics....*
>
> Public Records Office of Northern Ireland

C   A Protestant farmer looks at the situation:

> *On Tuesday night last I viewed the whole situation from midnight till 4 a.m. from a high hilltop.... Signals were being*

exchanged by the Sinn Feiners all along the Sperrins with their friends who were murdering the police in Bellaghy etc.... Is the government going to protect us and remove the danger?.... If the answer is 'No' the people here will defend themselves....

Belfast Newsletter, 6 May 1922

D Police report on occurrences on the night of 15 April 1921:

9.10 Special Sergeant (not on duty) James Davis at Finaghy Cross Roads was informed that four suspicious-looking men were proceeding from Lower Finaghy.

9.50 Reserve Patrol despatched from Dunmurry Station...took cover. Four suspicious men appeared on the footpath. The patrol held them up and took revolvers, wire cutters and papers from them and marched them to Dunmurry Barracks.

Quoted in P. Buckland's book, *Ulster Unionism... 1886–1922*, 1973

1 Do sources **A** and **B** provide any evidence that the Protestants were conducting a pogrom?

2 Does source **D** prove that the Specials did their job well?

3 Do any of the sources help to explain why some Protestants adopted the tactics described in source **B**?

The Special Powers Act

The treaty of 6 December 1921, which recognised the 26 southern counties as the Irish Free State, also set up the six northern counties as a separate state with its own parliament at Stormont. Sir James Craig became the first Prime Minister of the new state of Northern Ireland. Many southern politicians, however, still claimed that Ulster should be part of the Irish Free State, and the IRA continued its guerilla war in the north. To try to counter this, the northern government passed the Special Powers Act in 1922. This allowed internment (imprisonment without trial). Section 2 (4) said it was an offence '...if any person does any act of such a nature as to be calculated to be prejudicial to the preservation of the peace or maintenance of order in Northern Ireland'. By mid-1922 some 500 people, mostly Catholics, had been interned.

During the first half of 1922 the IRA mounted a major campaign in the north. The events listed in *The Times* for just one day – Tuesday 21 March 1922 – give an idea of the extent of the violence:

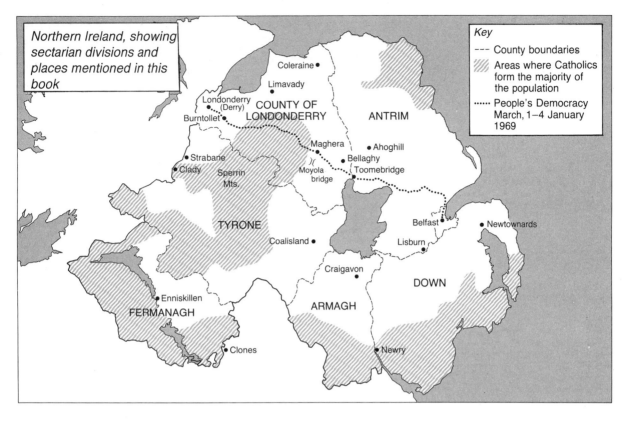

Northern Ireland, showing sectarian divisions and places mentioned in this book

Key
--- County boundaries
/// Areas where Catholics form the majority of the population
..... People's Democracy March, 1–4 January 1969

Orangeman: a member of the Protestant Orange order, named after William of Orange (see page 25)

flour mills: most industry in N. Ireland was Protestant-owned

Protestants at Coalisland attacked by a party of 30 IRA.
Party of Special Constables ambushed.
Maghera police barracks raided.
Bridge blown up at Moyola.
Special shot dead.
An Orangeman and a Special attacked, the former shot dead.
Two separate shootings in Belfast, one dead, one wounded.
N. Londonderry flour mills burned to the ground.
Telegraph wires cut, telegraph poles cut down, bridges blown up in N. Londonderry.

The Times editorial for that day was headed 'Ulster in Peril'.

The Protestants retaliated. Sectarian killings (killings for religion) reached a climax. When two policemen were shot by the IRA in March 1922, armed Specials lined up a Catholic family in their Belfast front room and shot five of them dead. In June 1922 a Protestant mob poured petrol over a Catholic doctor's housekeeper and tried to burn her alive.

In the two years leading up to July 1922, 428 people were killed. Out of the 93 000 Catholics living in Belfast, 257 were killed, 8750 lost their jobs, 23 000 were driven from their homes, and 500 Catholic shops and businesses were destroyed. The IRA offensive petered out by the end of 1922. The new state had survived.

Catholics flee to Dublin from Protestant violence in Belfast, in 1922. What makes this photograph especially touching?

Using the evidence: different perceptions

A   On 11 February there was an extraordinary incident. A platoon of sixteen armed A Specials left their depot at Newtonards for Enniskillen. They took a train which travelled through Co. Monaghan in the 26 counties and at Clones station some of them got out. Their presence in the 26 counties was completely illegal and they were challenged by the local commandant of the IRA, which was now the security force in the south. The Specials shot him dead and then the IRA guard in the station opened fire killing four. . . .

   The next day the Loyalists in Belfast took their revenge. . . . In one incident a bomb was thrown into a group of Catholic children in Weaver Street. . .killing six of them.
   M. Farrell: *Northern Ireland: The Orange State*, 1976

B   On 11 February a party of eighteen Ulster Special Constables, six of them armed, were on their way from the training camp at Newtonards, Co. Down, to Enniskillen. The only direct route by rail ran a short way through Free State territory, and involved changing trains at Clones, in Co. Monaghan, a few hundred yards from the border. Here they clashed with members of the I.R.A., a clash during which the I.R.A. commander and four special constables were killed. These events roused excitement on both sides to fever pitch. . .people being especially infuriated by the hurling of a bomb in Weaver Street where children were playing.
   P. Buckland: *Ulster Unionism. . .1886–1922*, 1973

C Events of May 1922, taken from *The Times*:

May 8 Border clash between Specials and IRA at Clady, County Tyrone.
10 Protestants shoot three Catholic brothers.
13 Robert Beattie, Protestant postman and Orangeman, shot dead. Patrol of B-Specials ambushed.
16 Shots fired at Beattie's funeral; the crowd chases and kills a suspect.
18 Two Catholics shot on a tramcar.
19 Three Protestants killed. Six factories set on fire by IRA. Catholic village burned down.
20 Country houses burned by IRA. Eleven Catholics killed and 220 Catholic families driven out.
22 Shooting of Unionist MP, W.J. Twaddell.
23 The Ulster government outlaws Sinn Fein. Two hundred Catholics interned.
26 Twelve fires started by the IRA in Protestant firms etc. A Catholic hotel porter disappears.
28 The IRA invades West Fermanagh. Pitched battle with 50 Specials. Border clash at Clady. Fires in Belfast.
31 Special shot in Belfast. Street of 86 Catholic houses burned down.

1 In what ways do sources **A** and **B** differ in their account of the Clones incident?

2 Does the fact that accounts differ imply a deliberate attempt to deceive the reader? Do sources **A** and **B** provide any evidence of an intention to mislead?

3 Are biased accounts useless to the historian?

4 Write two accounts of the events of May 1922, the first as Farrell would have written, the second as Buckland would have written. Check your answers against Appendix II on page 69.

The Thirties

The 1930s were a time of danger for the Unionist government. In 1932 Eamonn de Valera, who had promised 'to combat the exercise of any foreign authority in Ireland', was elected Prime Minister of Eire. It seemed to Unionist politicians that Ulster was under attack.

There was terrible economic depression; 28 per cent of the working population were unemployed in 1932, supported only by a humiliating system of dole. Worst hit of all were the Protestant skilled industrial workers in the dockyards and engineering firms.

The Northern Ireland Labour Party (NILP), which stressed working-class unity, grew more powerful.

On 4 October 1932 more than 500 men on the unemployment relief scheme in Belfast went on strike for more pay. There were demonstrations and riots in both Catholic and Protestant areas. On 11 October the police clashed with strikers in the Catholic Falls Road area of Belfast. An eye witness described what happened next:

> *On the Shankill Road [a Protestant area] crowds of growling men lounged around waiting...suddenly a big red-faced woman...ran to the crowds of men and, in quite terse language, told them that the unemployed and police were in conflict on the Falls Road. 'Are you'se going to let them down?' she almost shrieked. 'No by heavens we are not,' they roared back, and in almost a twinkling a veritable orgy of destruction began....*
>
> *There was consternation in the ranks of professional politicians....*
>
> J.J. Kelly: *A Journalist's Diary*, 1944

consternation: worry

The danger for the Unionist government lay in the unity of Catholic and Protestant workers. If the Protestant working class stopped voting Unionist, then the Unionist government might fall. Protestant leaders believed that:

> *These unfortunate conditions were used as a cloak by the communist Sinn Fein to attempt to start a revolution in our Province. We also greatly deplore that some of our loyal Protestant unemployed were misled to such an extent that they associated themselves with the enemies of their faith and principles.*
>
> *Belfast Newsletter*, 15 October 1932

On Friday 14 October the government gave way. Unemployment relief was trebled, and the strikers returned to work three days later.

Government ministers tried to split the Catholic and Protestant workers. Sir Basil Brooke (later to become Prime Minister) urged Unionist employers to give preference to Protestants:

> *Roman Catholics...were out with all their force and might to destroy the power and constitution of Ulster. There was a definite plot to overpower the vote of Unionists in the North. He would appeal to Loyalists therefore wherever possible to employ good Protestant lads and lassies (Cheers).... [Catholics] had got too many appointments, for men who were really out to cut their throats if the opportunity arose (Hear, hear).*
>
> Speech by Sir Basil Brooke reported in the *Fermanagh Times*, 13 July 1933

A Belfast 'character' of the 1940s. What can a historian learn from a photograph such as this?

When trouble flared up again in 1935, it consisted to a much greater degree of Protestant mobs attacking Catholic areas. The Unionist government had survived.

Questions

1 Examine de Valera's statement on page 11. Which is the most important word? Why?

2 Examine Sir Basil Brooke's speech, then explain how it was designed to turn Protestant working-class opinion against the Catholics.

Votes, housing and jobs

In 1920 there were more Unionists than Nationalists in Ulster. Protestants controlled the Northern Ireland Parliament at Stormont, most local councils, and many businesses. As Craig said in 1934: 'All I boast is that we have a Protestant Parliament and a Protestant state.'

Ulster local elections were not based on 'one man, one vote'. Only ratepayers could take part in elections; they were given one vote for every £10 rateable value up to a maximum of seven. This meant that in Londonderry wealthy Protestant businessmen could allocate seven votes, but 21 644 of the Catholics (who were generally poorer than Protestants) had no vote at all. Neither, on the other hand, did 8908 poor Protestants. To the Unionists, this seemed only fair. As businessmen, they paid most of the rates and provided most of the employment.

In 1923 a commission set up by Craig organised a system called 'gerrymandering' – changing electoral boundaries to rig an artificial

A divided city: Londonderry, showing the Catholic cathedral (left), the Protestant cathedral (right) and the Bogside (a Catholic area) beyond

Unionist majority. Londonderry provides one of the best examples of how gerrymandering worked. The Cameron Commission, set up by the Northern Ireland government in 1969 to investigate complaints, found that the city was divided into three wards:

Gerrymandering in Londonderry

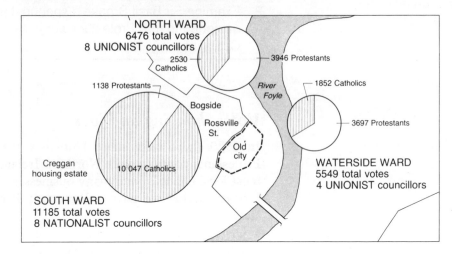

Another thing that the Unionists did, in 1929, was to abolish proportional representation. Proportional representation is a voting system whereby each constituency returns a number of candidates representing all the different parties, in proportion to the number of votes each party won. The British government had introduced it in 1920 to safeguard the position of the Catholic minority. Because proportional representation was abolished, by the end of the 1930s only two towns of any importance (Newry and Strabane) were under Nationalist control. Also, at the Northern Ireland Parliament at Stormont there were never more than a handful of Nationalist MPs (10 out of 52 in 1925, for example). The Unionists dealt with them quite simply:

> *Whenever [the Nationalists] rose to address the House, the Prime Minister and other ministers and many of their followers retired ostentatiously and deliberately to the smoke-room...scorned inferiority was stamped on the brows of one third of the area's population.*
>
> Irish News, 7 November 1932

ostentatiously: making a deliberate display

The Unionists, therefore, dominated business and politics. Many Loyalists saw the purpose of the new state as being to preserve the Protestant way of life. Historians have claimed that they used their power in industry and government to give preference to their own supporters in the years up to 1968. The Cameron Commission found 'abundant evidence' of discrimination against Catholics, not only in election arrangements, but also in the employment of government and council officials, and in council housing. It also found that the Royal Ulster Police (RUC) were guilty of 'misjudgements' and

Londonderry in 1955: one person in five was unemployed. How might this have made the sectarian situation more dangerous?

circumspect: careful

'misconduct'. Eamonn McCann, a Catholic who grew up in Londonderry, explained the Catholic view of the system:

> *It was accepted that the Unionists were responsible for unemployment. New industries which came to Northern Ireland were directed to the Protestant centres in the east.... The Unionist tactic, we believed, was designed to compel a disproportionate number of Catholics to leave Northern Ireland and thereby to preserve the Protestant majority....*
>
> *The housing situation too was very bad.... Only householders could vote at local government elections. To give a person a house, therefore, was to give him a vote, and the Unionist Party in Derry had to be very circumspect about the people to whom it gave votes. It would have been political suicide for it to have given Catholics houses and votes outside the South Ward where most Derry Catholics were corralled. So houses were built on a bleak hill, Creggan, overlooking the Bogside....*
>
> *When building land in the South Ward began to run short the Corporation was faced with the problem of either housing Catholics in other wards or not housing them at all. It opted for the latter.*
>
> E. McCann: *War and an Irish Town,* 1974

The effect of this discrimination was to reinforce the differences between Catholics and Protestants. The Unionists simply built the divisions into Ulster's institutions. Social and religious ill-feeling was entrenched in government, employment and housing structures. When, after 1968, the government tried to heal the rift between the Catholics and the Protestants, it was to find that sectarian hostility was too deeply engrained in the fabric of the state.

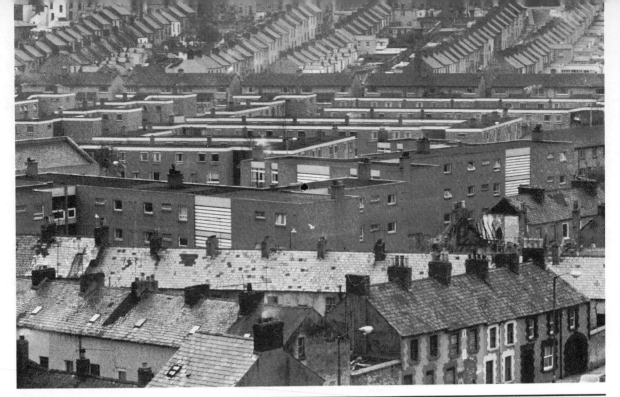

Catholic Bogside district of Londonderry. Rossville Street (see page 41) is just behind the new Rossville flats in the foreground

Questions

1 Using the map of Londonderry on page 14, explain clearly how gerrymandering worked.

2 Nationalist politicians eventually withdrew from the Stormont Parliament. Debate whether or not they made the right decision.

3 Gerrymandering is unacceptable to people used to English politics. The Nationalists, however, were not an English opposition party. If they had ever won a majority, they would have taken Northern Ireland out of the United Kingdom. Were the Unionists, therefore, justified in gerrymandering the boundaries to make sure this never happened? Had they any alternatives?

Using the evidence: how much discrimination?

A *Where one man's religion is another's passport to a job....*
A newspaper article listed a number of examples of discrimination against Catholics applying for council jobs in Armagh, including:

CANDIDATE A: for the job of council recreation officer
Name   Timothy Duffy
Education   Belfast College of Technology, University of Loughborough, Ulster College Northern Ireland Polytechnic.

Examinations National Examination Board in Supervisory Management, Diploma in Supervisory Management, Recreation Management Certificate, Diploma in Management Studies, 3rd, 2nd and 1st class Certificates in Turf Culture and Sports Ground Management.
Member British Institute of Management, Institute of Supervisory Management, Association of Recreation Management (Chairman of Northern Ireland Branch), Institute of Groundsmanship.
Experience Assistant Recreation Tourist Officer
He didn't get the job: he's a Catholic.

CANDIDATE B: for the same job: recreation officer
Name   William Morton
Education   Left school at 14
Examinations None
Member   Institute of Groundsmanship, Northern Ireland Industrial Safety Group
Experience Gardener, Landscape supervisor
He got the job: he's a Protestant.

Sunday Times, 8 March 1981

B Job advertisements from Ulster newspapers in the 1960s:

WANTED – man and woman to look after two cows, both Protestants.

Wanted – Reliable cook-general, Protestant (Christian preferred).

C A recent study

Much of the data concerning alleged discrimination by the state and state institutions in Northern Ireland has been provided by political pressure groups. The quality has been very uneven; conflicting evidence is sometimes ignored, sources are often omitted and particular anecdotes used to claim general points....

John Darby: *Conflict in Northern Ireland*, 1976

anecdotes: stories

1 Do sources **A** and **B** prove that there was widespread discrimination against Catholics in Northern Ireland? Explain your answer.

2 What can historians learn from source **C**?

2 THE PROTESTANTS

Morris Fraser, a Belfast child psychologist, has studied the beliefs and actions of Protestants living in Northern Ireland. He thinks they can be explained by modern psychiatric theories about elite groups. An elite group believes that it is superior. To support this belief it has to find an 'out group' to despise. It then gives the out group a stereotyped character, which includes poverty, stupidity, dirtiness, over-breeding and superstition. If the out group retaliates violently, the elite group points out that this behaviour is typical. If the out group accepts its position, the elite group suggests that it actually enjoys being dirty and ignorant by nature (the 'contentment myth').

Orange march, 1972. What does this photograph tell the historian about the Orange order?

Using the evidence: extreme Protestants' opinions

Before you read this section, it must be stressed that the following extracts do not represent the views of all Protestants.

A The Orange character

An Orangeman should have... a humble and steadfast faith in Jesus Christ.... He should cultivate truth and justice, brotherly kindness and charity, devotion and piety, concord and unity and obedience to the laws; his deportment should be gentle and compassionate, kind and courteous... he should love, uphold and defend the Protestant religion.... He should strenuously oppose the fatal errors and doctrines of the Church of Rome....

Rev. Dr M.W. Dewar: *Why Orangeism?*, 1959

piety: religious behaviour
concord: agreement
deportment: behaviour

B God's chosen people

beads: rosary beads used by Catholics when praying

gods of stone: a reference to the statues of the Virgin Mary and the saints in Catholic churches

> *We want no Popish tyrant priest*
> *To guide us on our way;*
> *We know not how to count the beads,*
> *Such trash we throw away;*
> *To idols dumb and gods of stone,*
> *We'll never bend the knee,*
> *Nor say confessions in the dark;*
> *Our consciences are free.*
>   *Crimson Banner Song Book*, 1975

C Two Protestant jokes

Strasbourg: the European Court of Human Rights

> In one joke an IRA man is pictured talking to another:
>   *Here is a letter to Strasbourg telling how the British torture us every morning.*
>   *Torture us? How?*
>   *They make us wash, don't they?...*

In the other a Belfast Republican docker is walking along the quay kicking a tortoise.
   A policeman asks: Why are you kicking that poor defenceless tortoise?
   Rebel: It's been following me around all day.
                Quoted in G. Bell's book,
                The Protestants of Ulster, 1978

D Description of IRA gunman

> Rank Status of the I-Ran-Away army
> Qualifications   Non-worker, large family, can quote [social security] rules backwards, under 5ft 2in.
> Uniform   Felt hat, dirty raincoat, running shoes.
> Habits   Washes once a year, whether dirty or not.
> Points of   Two yellow streaks down back, kicks cats
> Recognition   and old ladies when really angry....
>   *Loyalist News*, 20 March 1971

E A Protestant view of Southern Ireland

> *Fear of committing supposed sins,...unhappy marriages arising from...the inferior position given to women...and many other social and personal handicaps, seem to make citizens of the Irish Republic unhappy and inadequate.*
>   *A major evidence of this is the extent to which citizens of the Republic seek to drown their sorrows in alcohol....*
>   *Many of us Ulster Protestants regard the Irish Republic as a very sick country...the Irish Republic is the place of origin*

of many extremists, people unable to settle down to any form of stable, public-spirited and responsible living.
Rev. W. Martyn Smith, *Sectarianism – Roads to Reconciliation*, 1974

F Fighting the Catholics

*I was born under the Union Jack,
I was born under the Union Jack,
If guns are made for shooting,
Then skulls are made to crack.
You've never seen a better Taig,
Than with a bullet in his back.*
Orange Loyalist Songs, 1971

Taig: Catholic

7 September 1971: the funeral of a Catholic baby, Angela Gallagher, killed by a terrorist bullet

1 Make a list of the ways in which the Protestants in the sources think and talk about Catholics.

2 Do the sources support Morris Fraser's psychiatric theory that the Ulster Protestants are a typical elite group?

The Rev. Dr Ian Kyle Paisley

Ian Paisley started his own Free Presbyterian Church in 1951. His doctorate is an honorary degree from an American Bible College. Yet he has had a great influence on Ulster Protestants. When David Armstrong heard him speak in 1964:

Mr Paisley spoke about Jesus Christ, explaining from the Bible who Jesus was, and what he had done...so that instead of eternal death we should be able to have a relationship with God and be with him for ever.
The Rev. David Armstrong: *A Road Too Wide*, 1985

Dr Paisley is violently critical of Roman Catholicism. When the Archbishop of Canterbury visited the Pope, Paisley charged him with 'high treason against this realm'. In his writings he has suggested that 'popery' is of the devil; that Roman Catholicism is attended by murder, theft, immorality, lust and incest; and that the Roman Catholic Church, the Communists and the Jews have formed a worldwide anti-Protestant plot to destroy Ulster.

British churchmen and politicians, he says, do not properly understand the situation. They have been tricked into becoming part of

Paisley on the hustings in 1969

the plot. He criticised the group of ministers who met IRA men at Feakle in 1974 to try to persuade them to stop terrorism:

> *We fight for our lives and for our national identity.... The Lord will not deliver Ulster while her people do not realize that there are...those fickle, Feakle clergy who would lead the Protestants of Ulster astray.*
>
> Irish Times, 27 January 1975

Paisley is one of the 'loyal rebels' of Ulster, who are prepared to resist the British government in order to stay part of Britain.

> *Our fathers rejected the attempts of the British Parliament, swayed by the Irish Nationalists, to force home rule on Ireland. If the Crown in Parliament decreed to put Ulster into a United Ireland, we would be disloyal to Her Majesty if we did not resist such a surrender to our enemies.*
>
> Irish Times, 7 July 1975

Dr Paisley first came to public notice in October 1956, when it was alleged that he had helped a 15-year-old Catholic girl, who had become a Protestant, to run away from home. In 1966 he started publishing a weekly paper, the *Protestant Telegraph*, to prevent Protestants being tricked, as he saw it, away from the truth. Also in the 1960s he set up the 'Protestant Unionist Party', which in 1971 was re-organised into the Democratic Unionist Party (DUP).

Despite his strongly held views, the Rev. Paisley is, however, known as an effective MP and Euro-MP, who works hard to solve the housing and unemployment problems of both Protestants and Catholics in his constituency.

Question

It is often claimed that Protestants living in Northern Ireland have a 'siege mentality' (sometimes called a 'fortress mentality') – they act, and react, as though there is a constant conspiracy to destroy them. Identify all the ways in which Paisley appeals to this 'siege mentality'.

Using the evidence: opinions of Paisley

A The right man to save Ulster?

> *I think Dr Ian Paisley is the right man to save Ulster from civil war. He is a straightforward man and always comes to the point. I think he is the reincarnation of St Patrick who is believed to have banished the snakes out of Ireland. It*

appears that a few got away and God has chosen Dr Paisley to finish the job. There are many Roman Catholics who were opposed to Dr Paisley earlier on but now have changed their minds because they have discovered that Dr Paisley is a God-fearing man and a Christian gentleman.

B A vicious bigot?

bigot: someone with a closed mind

As Ian Paisley is once again showing his true colours as the vicious bigot that he is, perhaps it is prudent to remember it was the Catholic community that asked the British government to send in troops to protect them from the Protestant-backed 'B-Specials' and the Ulster Defence Association.

   I can see no difference between the religious apartheid of Northern Ireland and the racial apartheid of South Africa. They are both obscene.

   As Paisley considers himself a Christian (a fact which I doubt very much) he ought to revise his Ten Commandments. He's forgotten one – Love Thy Neighbour.

C Pure evil?

blasphemy: insulting God

I entered [Rev. Paisley's church] perfectly prepared to find that Mr Paisley, too, has a good side. . . . Yet when I left the place an hour and a half later I knew that I had been in the presence of pure evil. . . . I was aware of blasphemy being committed as this demented creature paced from end to end of his pulpit-stage, flourishing the Bible and repetitively – almost hypnotically – insisting on the need to defend, to fight, to do battle, to vanquish, to conquer, to assert, to unsheath the sword, to show no mercy to the enemies of God. . . . One young man, sitting on my left in the next seat, twisted his folded hands until his knuckles cracked at each exhortation to go forth and attack the anti-Christ.

D A real Irishman?

O'Neill: Prime Minister of Northern Ireland, 1963–9

O'Neill was pussy-footin' about trying to keep Paisley calm. He was a fool of a Prime Minister. . . . Too much namby-pamby Eton carry-on. That kinda crap's no good in Belfast. . . . Paisley could knock him flat with a look – and often did. He's bad news, Paisley. But at least he's a real Irishman.

1 Deduce which of the passages was written by:
   a) an Englishwoman;
   b) a Southern Irish Catholic, very moderate;

c) an Ulster Protestant;
d) a Catholic IRA member.
Explain your choices. The answers are in Appendix III on page 70.

2 Identify the literary techniques used by the writer of source C to make the reader
a) dislike Paisley;
b) fear Paisley.

Belfast pedalabouts – mostly Orange

In June 1976 a Catholic journalist from Southern Ireland, Dervla Murphy, rode north on her bicycle. After a year in Northern Ireland, talking to people on both sides, she was very critical of many Protestants:

xenophobia: fear of foreigners

> *The Orange tradition is an uncouth mixture of ignorance, xenophobia, self-deception, suspicion, rabble-rousing, fear and aggression. Inevitably this produces a great deal of loutish behaviour, which its leaders seem unwilling or unable to correct. One example is the custom of calling a football 'The Pope' and ritually kicking it around a field. Some outsiders find this funny but I am not amused.*
>
> Dervla Murphy: *A Place Apart*, 1978

Protestant homes in a Belfast ghetto. The occupants set fire to their homes, rather than let Catholics take them over

Yet for all this, Mrs Murphy's accounts of the Protestants she met are sympathetic and understanding. She blames the politicians for

Protestant ghetto: an area, usually of poor housing, inhabited only by Protestants

misleading the people:

> *If Belfast's Protestant ghetto dwellers do look dour and grey they have every excuse; and who can blame them if they are easily provoked to fear-inspired violence? They have been reared on a diet of ignorance, aggression, suspicion, misunderstanding, superstition and dread – dread that the Catholics will outbreed them, and get their jobs, and perhaps marry their children and turn their grandchildren into Papists. Scorning these people for bigotry is about as reasonable as scorning a cat for killing birds.*

The theme of the kindness, even goodness, of the average Protestant recurs throughout the book:

> *...almost without exception I found him polite, kind, generous, helpful and welcoming...not at all the dour, hard-headed, thick-skinned, unimaginative character one had been conditioned to expect.*
>
> *There are many Orange clergymen whom it is a privilege to meet because of their sincerity, their unexpected and touching innocence, their real spirituality – in a word, their sheer goodness....*

On one occasion she was shocked to meet a man who had lost an eye. A young mother with a tiny baby under her arm had attacked him with a knife while he poured petrol over her furniture during a sectarian riot. The story 'sickened' her, but:

> *I found him very friendly and perfectly willing to help a Southerner named Murphy. In no way did he resemble the type one visualises when thinking of mobs savagely rioting.... I've been with the IRA, the UDA, the Orangemen – and where are all the ogres, the evil influences, the brutal thugs? They must be somewhere but I've not met them....*

Dervla Murphy came to the conclusion that the problem of Northern Ireland was 'the use of labels':

> *When people are thought of only as Prods or Taigs, Unionists or Republicans, Orangemen or Papists, then it must become impossible to judge them on their individual merits as human beings.*

The Plews family's home in Fountain Street (Protestant area of Londonderry), photographed in the 1960s. Mrs Dorothy Plews' daughter Edith (sitting) married a Roman Catholic. What difficulties would you expect for such a marriage?

Questions

1. Dervla Murphy suggests that 'labelling' might be at the root of the Northern Ireland problem. From what you have read so far, choose two examples of labelling in statements made by Unionist politicians. In both your examples, explain how this labelling is unjust.

2. Identify other groups which are often similarly caricatured.

Using the evidence: when extremism is necessary

Most Northern Ireland Protestants are 'decent Christians, neighbourly, and advocates of liberty'. They have been British Loyalists for three centuries, proving it with their blood on the battlefields of Europe. They keep calm after even the most horrific atrocities: when terrorists machine-gunned Pentecostal Christians at worship in Darkley Chapel, Co. Antrim, on 21 November 1983, killing three people, the congregation invited them to return, so they could tell the killers that they forgave them.

Above all they are 'distressed' by the criticism of them expressed by many British people and by the sympathy apparently given to the IRA. Here are some of the arguments they use to explain why they want a firmer line against the IRA in Northern Ireland:

A   An extremist

*An extremist is a person who holds his faith extremely,
This point of view to timid folk might appear unseemly,
But timid folk did not come forth when extremists did enjoin,
To fight alongside William at the Battle of the Boyne.*

*In the Ulster crisis an arch extremist, Sir Edward, took the reins,
And the Covenant was signed in blood from many an extremist's veins,
Fronted by an Empire they defiantly stood their ground,
Whilst as usual the timid folk were in hiding to be found.*

*So when Ulster is in danger the extremist will take a hand,
Because they have an extreme love towards their native land,
A faith, a Crown and a way of life they'll never sacrifice,
But fight like loyal Ulstermen and not timid ULSTER MICE.*
           'Gusty' Spence: *Orange Loyalist Songs*, 1971

B   Can you ignore a revolution?

It is scarcely conceivable [that] large parts of Birmingham or Manchester would have been allowed for months on end [to remain in a state of rebellion].

What is essential to defeating a revolution...is the will for victory....

Had Britain concentrated single-mindedly on [defeating the IRA], the battle in Ulster would now be over.
           T. E. Utley: *Lessons of Ulster*, 1975

Orange parade. Note the banner showing William of Orange

William: King William of Orange, who put down the 1689 rebellion at the Battle of the Boyne in 1690. His troops ran their gun carriages over the wounded Irish

Sir Edward: Sir Edward Carson, the first Unionist leader

The Sandy Row district of Belfast prepares for the Orange marching season. How can you tell that this is a Protestant area? List at least five clues

C When fears seem proven

Perhaps more sympathy might be felt outside Ireland for the Ulster Protestants if it were generally realised that Article 2 of the Republic's Constitution states: 'The national territory consists of the whole island of Ireland. . . .'

This claim reinforces the Ulster Protestants' fears and encourages them to think the Republic is working secretly with Westminster to bring it about.

Robert G. Crawford: *Loyal to King Billy*, 1987

D Shoot-to-kill

There's no such thing as arresting people, or detaining people who have rocket launchers, rifles, pistols and other weapons of death. Now I know the option I want – I want to see them dead. They've got to be killed, or we're going to have another 16 years like we've had before. . . .

I think that all those who have lost their loved ones, all those who are grieving, would take it as a grievous insult if anyone were to sit down with people who planned and executed the murder of their loved ones. . . . What they want is those people dealt with – to see effective action taken against the IRA.

Something has to be done, there's got to be something that will finish the trouble once and for all – and the only way you do that with the IRA is to kill them.

Gregory Campbell, Democratic Unionist Politician, speaking on the BBC *Real Lives* programme, 1985

1. Identify from sources **A–D** the arguments that Protestants use when proposing a tougher policy in Northern Ireland.

2. In July 1966 Ian Paisley was sent to jail for 'unlawful assembly and breach of peace'. Subsequently, on 22 July, a 4000-strong Protestant march attacked Catholic areas. Using the knowledge you have gained from this book so far, write an essay describing the thoughts and feelings that might have led a Protestant to take part in the riot.

The UDA (the Protestant terrorist Ulster Defence Association) in action. What can the historian learn about the UDA from these three photographs?

3 REFORM

O'Neill and Wilson

Before World War II most Catholics in Northern Ireland hated the new state, and simply looked forward to a time when Ulster would be re-united as part of Eire. This changed after 1945.

> *Don't quote me, but we are changing our minds. We now think that we would like to stay in the United Kingdom....*
>
> Anonymous Catholic quoted by
> Terence O'Neill in *The Times*, 1 January 1969

> *Compulsory national insurance, increased family allowances and the Health Service all helped to shield Catholics from the worst effects of unemployment and poverty.... And since such benefits were not available south of the border the tendency to regard the achievement of a united Ireland as the only way to make things better began to weaken.*
>
> E. McCann: *War and an Irish Town*, 1974

south of the border: in Eire

Consequently, when the IRA renewed their guerilla campaign in 1956 it was a failure, and in 1962 they had to abandon it. An IRA statement blamed:

> *...the attitude of the general public whose minds have been deliberately distracted from the supreme issue facing the Irish people – the unity and freedom of Ireland.*
>
> Quoted in J.B. Bell's book, *The Secret Army: a History of the IRA*, 1972

In the 1961 elections, just 73 000 people voted Nationalist (equivalent to only 15 per cent of the Catholic population, although it must be pointed out that Nationalist candidates stood in only 11 of the 52 constituencies – those with a Catholic majority).

At the same time, Unionists seemed to be changing. Many were critical of the Ulster Prime Minister, Lord Brookeborough (formerly Sir Basil Brooke), and in 1963 he resigned. His successor, Terence O'Neill, was a Protestant but said that he wanted to 'break the chains of ancient hatreds'. O'Neill was supported by the English Prime Minister, Harold Wilson:

the minority: the Catholics

> *I was anxious that the Ulster Unionist government under Captain O'Neill should be encouraged to press on with their programme of...improving the lot of the minority of Northern Ireland. Since coming into office he had, by Northern Ireland standards, carried through a remarkable programme of easement.*
>
> H. Wilson: *The Labour Government*, 1971

The British government injected £450 million into the Ulster economy, built motorways and a new university, and attracted new industries. Economic and cultural links were established with Southern Ireland. In January and February 1965 O'Neill met the Irish Prime Minister, Sean Lemass. 'Gusty' Spence and two other Protestants were imprisoned for the murder of two Catholics.

O'Neill's measures were not welcomed by all Unionists. In September there was an attempt to replace him as leader, which involved half the Unionists at Stormont. Nevertheless, in the late sixties, it seemed to many people that Ulster's hatreds were beginning to heal.

Mr and Mrs Terence O'Neill outside Stormont in 1963

Using the evidence: Terence O'Neill

A *Protestant girl required for housework. Apply to the Hon. Mrs Terence O'Neill, Glebe House, Ahoghill, Co. Antrim.*
        Advertisement in the *Belfast Telegraph,* November 1959

B *If you give Roman Catholics a good job and a good house they will live like Protestants, because they will see neighbours with cars and television sets. They will refuse to have eighteen children. But if the Roman Catholic is jobless and lives in a most ghastly hovel, he will rear eighteen children on National Assistance.... If you treat Roman Catholics with due consideration and kindness they will live like Protestants in spite of the authoritative nature of their religion.*
        Terence O'Neill speaking on the radio, May 1969

C *Orangeism marks a man for life. By all accounts Lord O'Neill is an intelligent, well-meaning and honourable man who felt so strongly about civil rights for Catholics that he sacrificed his political career in an attempt to secure them.... His remarks betrayed that however sincere his dedication to the cause of justice for the minority – and nobody ever seriously questioned its sincerity – he simply cannot regard Catholics as fully paid-up members of the human race.*
        Dervla Murphy: *A Place Apart,* 1978

D *Unionism led by Captain O'Neill has been given its instructions by its British masters, to make itself more respectable, to brush discrimination, gerrymandering and bigotry under the table.*
        Republican Manual of Education, Part 2, 1972

E *Conscious of his political weakness...O'Neill was making the main plank of his premiership the improvement of*

community relations...but the methods he used were not always helpful to the cause. Flamboyant gestures were no substitute for real action, and only raised hopes that were not being fulfilled....
Brian Faulkner: *Memoirs of a Statesman*, 1978

1 Why, in your opinion, did one historian describe O'Neill's speech (source B) as 'stupefying in its tone of condescension'?

2 Do you agree with Dervla Murphy that O'Neill was sincere? What alternatives are suggested to you by the sources?

Civil liberties

Although many Catholics welcomed O'Neill's reforms, others became disillusioned. Economic investment seemed to be concentrated in the Protestant eastern part of the Province. The new industrial centre was named, provocatively, Craigavon, after Ulster's first prime minister. The new university was sited, not in Londonderry, but in Protestant Coleraine.

No attempt has been made by the Northern Ireland Government to knit the community together; there have been no electoral reforms.... Not merely has Captain O'Neill dashed the hopes he himself raised, he has added a new bitterness and disappointment to the grievances of the minority.
NI Labour Party, *Election Manifesto*, 1965

Bernadette Devlin. Does this photograph help to explain Miss Devlin's appeal to Catholics?

In February 1967 the Northern Ireland Civil Rights Association (NICRA) was formed. It demanded one-man-one-vote, the end of gerrymandering, an end to discrimination in jobs and housing, and the disbanding of the B-Specials. It was supported by a student movement called the People's Democracy, whose members included Bernadette Devlin and Eamonn McCann. To many British people NICRA seemed a moderate body asking for reasonable reforms. In 1969 the Cameron Commission reported that:

non-sectarian: it rejected the old politics based on religion

The Civil Rights Association maintained that it was non-sectarian and concerned only with obtaining reforms and changes in the law, which it sought always by peaceful and non-violent means.
Command Paper 532: *Disturbances in Northern Ireland*,
September 1969

Protestants, however, were more cynical:

Bernadette Devlin and her associates had a firm reputation in Britain as the moderate representatives of an oppressed minority.

Does this photograph help to explain why Miss Devlin was popular in England?

> *The fact that their declared aim was the total destruction of the existing political institutions...passed unnoticed.... The origin of the Civil Rights Movement itself was a private discussion in Londonderry in August [sic] 1967 at which...the Commander-in-Chief of the Official IRA was present....*
>
> T.E. Utley: *Lessons of Ulster*, 1975

The Association used what it called 'direct action'. It organised marches, squatted in newly built council houses, and disrupted traffic and council meetings. On Saturday 5 October 1968, the Association held a march in Londonderry itself. Traditionally only Protestants had marched within the city walls, and the RUC had

Civil Rights march, 1969. Make a list of the demands on the banners

banned the march. Television viewers in Britain were shocked to see the 'very disappointing crowd' of a few hundred marchers attacked by the police:

> ...Men, women and children were clubbed to the ground. People were fleeing down the street from the front cordon [of police] and up the street from the rear cordon, crashing into one another, stumbling over one another, huddling in doorways, some screaming....
> E. McCann: *War and an Irish Town*, 1974

Bernadette Devlin later claimed that the police attack helped the movement: 'They gave it life in one day.' When on 16 November 1968 another march was organised over the same route, 15 000 people turned up. On 22 November O'Neill announced a package of reforms which met all the Association's demands except one-man-one-vote. Many moderates in the Civil Rights Movement welcomed the reforms, and supported O'Neill's television appeal for calm.

Burntollet

In spite of O'Neill's appeal, at the start of 1969 the People's Democracy decided to maintain the pressure on the government by organising a march from Belfast to Londonderry (Derry).

Events of the march

1 Jan. Eighty marchers left Belfast. Police transported them by car past a hostile crowd of more than one hundred people at the County Antrim boundary.

2 Jan. The police transported the marchers round a hostile Protestant demonstration near Toomebridge. Some local supporters carrying a Republican flag joined the march. Eventually the police transported them to Maghera. Protestants rioted in Maghera. The marchers were protected by the local IRA, carrying shot-guns.

3 Jan. The police diverted the march around Maghera. There were by now some 500 marchers. They rejected police suggestions for further diversions, and marched straight towards Londonderry.

4 Jan. The police warned the marchers of possible trouble, but they decided to continue. Burntollet ambush. The march continued into Londonderry.

Based on the *Sunday Times* Insight team's book, *Ulster*, 1972

The march caused a political crisis in Northern Ireland. Eamonn McCann, who went on the march, commented:

> *The march was a horrific seventy-three-mile trek which dredged to the surface all the accumulated political filth of fifty Unionist*

Conflict at Burntollet Bridge. Does the chaos shown in this photograph influence your answer to question 4 in this section?

cudgel: stick

years.... *On the final day of the march, at Burntollet Bridge a few miles outside Derry, a force of some hundreds, marshalled by members of the B Specials and watched passively by our 'escort' of more than a hundred police, attacked with nailed clubs, stones and bicycle chains.*

E. McCann: *War and an Irish Town*, 1974

Michael Farrell, the march organiser, wrote bitterly:

There was no doubt it was a trap. The RUC knew an ambush had been prepared. Heaps of stones had been collected the night before and crowds of cudgel-wielding men had been gathering since early morning while RUC men stood among them laughing and chatting. During the ambush some of the RUC joined in and attacked the marchers too.... I remember going back to the bridge and finding RUC and ambushers sitting about relaxing. It later turned out that nearly a hundred of the ambush party were off-duty B Specials.

M. Farrell: *Northern Ireland: the Orange State*, 1976

Terence O'Neill, however, saw the march in a different light:

At best those who planned [the march] were careless of the effects which it would have. At worst they embraced with enthusiasm the prospect of...damage to the interests of Northern Ireland.... Some of the marchers and those who supported them in Londonderry itself have shown themselves to be mere hooligans ready to attack the police and others.

Statement made by Terence O'Neill, 5 January 1969

And after studying the events of the march, the Cameron Commission also criticised the marchers:

> *The members of the People's Democracy said they merely expected groups to come and say 'Boo' and 'Go Home'. Such naivety we find surprising....*
>
> *We are driven to think that the leaders [of the march] must have intended...to increase tension, so that in the process a more radical programme could be realised. They saw the march as a calculated martyrdom.*
>
> *We are convinced that a serious effort was made [by the police] to protect the marchers at Burntollet....*
>
> Command Paper 532: *Disturbances in Northern Ireland,*
> September 1969

The aftermath of Burntollet: rioting in Derry

When the marchers reached Londonderry, the Catholics rioted. That night the police roamed through the Bogside, damaging property and beating up Catholics.

O'Neill resigned on 28 April 1969, but Harold Wilson forced the Ulster government to introduce the reforms he had wanted: one-man-one-vote, and the disbanding of the B-Specials. Violence, however, continued. When the government allowed the traditional Protestant 'Apprentice Boys Parade' to go ahead in Londonderry on 12 August, Catholics in the Bogside prepared to protect themselves. They organised the Derry Citizens Defence Association, put up the barricades, flew Republican flags, and resisted police attacks for three days. On 14 August 1969 the first British troops arrived in Londonderry.

Questions

1. McCann and Farrell actually walked with the march. Does this make their accounts more reliable? Support your argument, wherever possible, with evidence from the sources.

2. In what ways does O'Neill's opinion differ from those of McCann and Farrell? Why do their interpretations differ?

3. The table of events on page 32 relates, as impartially as possible, the events of the march. After studying these facts, which opinion do you support, that of O'Neill, or that of McCann and Farrell?

4. How useful is memory as an historical source?

5. Writing in the late 1980s, the former Prime Minister James Callaghan commented: 'Looking back, I would fix the short period from 1963 to 1966 as the three years when Northern Ireland had its best chance to prevent the bombings and shootings of the 1970s and 1980s. But the chance was lost.' Why did the promise of the period 1963–6 dissolve into the violence of 1968–9?

'What are we doing to our children?' A youth throws a petrol bomb

4 VIOLENCE

Internment

The British troops brought only a few months of peace. In the summer of 1970 violence returned to Ulster. When the first Orange march of the season passed by the Catholic Ballymurphy area of Belfast, the Catholics rioted. The Army reacted violently, using CS gas for the first time in Northern Ireland. Many Catholics, who had believed that the Army would defend them, now said it was helping the Protestants to attack them.

Meanwhile, the IRA had re-organised, financed by a group of Eire businessmen and politicians (Charles Haughey, later Prime Minister of Eire, was implicated). A group calling itself the Provisional IRA (the Provos), dedicated to violent terrorism, broke away in November 1969. Soon afterwards they began a bombing campaign against shops, banks and electricity stations. On 6 February 1971 they were responsible for the death of the first British soldier in Ireland for nearly 50 years. In March 1971 three young Scottish soldiers were lured from a Belfast pub and executed.

By this time the Protestants were calling loudly for tougher measures against the IRA. James Chichester-Clark, who had followed O'Neill as Prime Minister, resigned. The Provo campaign mounted. In April there were 37 bombings, in May 47, in June 50, and in July 91. In August 1971 the new Ulster Prime Minister, Brian Faulkner, telephoned the British Prime Minister, Edward Heath. He told him that:

> *Not only was the increase of violence causing alarm.... The attacks...were preventing any kind of normal life in the Province. Simple things, like catching a bus or driving through the city to see a friend or going to the cinema, were becoming increasingly hazardous.... The message was beginning to come through that there was only one major unused weapon in the government's anti-terrorist arsenal – internment.*
>
> Brian Faulkner: *Memoirs of a Statesman*, 1978

arsenal: store of weapons
internment: imprisonment without trial

At 4.15 a.m. on Monday, 9 August 1971, 3000 troops moved in on Catholic areas all over the Province to arrest suspected IRA members. By the evening 342 people had been picked up.

The impact of internment

Internment created a fierce controversy. Imprisonment without trial is a breach of human rights. Faulkner realised the problems

Top: *six handcuffed internees are led from an RAF helicopter*

Above: *is this anti-internment march taking place in Belfast or London? Explain your answer*

involved, but he believed that the situation necessitated firm action:

> *I have taken this step solely for the protection of life and the security of property.... I ask those who will quite sincerely consider the use of internment powers as evil to answer honestly this question: is it more of an evil than to allow the perpetrators of these outrages to remain at liberty?*
>
> Brian Faulkner, Press statement, 9 August 1971

He misjudged the strength of opposition that internment would arouse. A 'Campaign for Social Justice' assembled hundreds of complaints of mistreatment, such as that of Henry Bennett of Belfast:

Aged: 25. Married with two children.... Worker in fertilizer factory.

At 3.45 a.m. on Monday 9th August 1971, four soldiers broke down my front door and came upstairs with guns at the ready. There were six soldiers outside.

I was told that I was being arrested under the Special Powers Act. I was given thirty seconds to get a towel and shaving kit into a sandbag which they gave me.

I said: 'I'm not the one you are looking for as I only moved into this house a couple of days ago.' I showed them a letter to identify myself. I was taken downstairs and made to lie prone on the floor while they radioed H.Q. A little while later they said: 'Come on, you'll do.' I was dressed in shirt, pants, one shoe and one sock. My other shoe and sock were in the sandbag.

I was thrown into a lorry and taken to Paulette Ave. They called me 'A Catholic b.....d'. They said 'You'll need more than medals and the Virgin Mary to save you....'

[At Girdwood Barracks].... About an hour and a half later I was taken by four military policemen along with four other prisoners. I was forced to run over broken glass and rough stones to a helicopter without shoes. I spent only 15 seconds in the helicopter and I was then pushed out into the hands of military policemen.

I was forced to crawl between these policemen back to the building. They kicked me on the hands, legs, ribs and kidney area. They threw me up the steps into the building, all the time they kept saying things like: 'You are good Catholic dogs and we are your masters.' As a result of their abuse I was injured on my sides and face....

I was taken to a room and questioned by two plain clothed detectives. I was told by one detective that I knew members of the I.R.A. in my district. I said that I didn't. I was accused of blowing up buildings. They claimed to have proof of this. I was also called a 'f.....g Republican sympathiser'. This detective left.

The other detective said: 'He is not nice but you need have no fear of me.' He promised me a generous weekly allowance and safe passage abroad if I gave him information about I.R.A. men....

I was released at noon the same day.... To the best of my knowledge the information which I have given above is a true and accurate account of what happened.

Signature: Henry Bennett
Witness: Rev. Brian J. Brady
Date: 14th August 1971

Campaign for Social Justice: *The Mailed Fist – A Record of Army Brutality*, 1971

medals: medallions of the saints, often valued by Catholics

There were claims of torture, which were later upheld by the European Court of Human Rights. For example:

The special helicopter torture, associated with Americans in Vietnam, was used at Girdwood on Monday morning. Bags were placed over prisoners' heads, after which they were bundled into helicopters which flew around for a time. They were then thrown out of the still-airborne machines. At this point, the helicopters were but a few feet off the ground, but as the prisoners would not have been aware of this, the mental torture suffered would have been tremendous.

Sunday Press, 15 August 1971

Internment, moreover, affected others besides those arrested. Their families suffered with them. One child psychologist reported:

A ten-year-old patient said: 'They came up the street at five in the morning, breaking windows. They jumped on our stairs and broke them. I screamed and jumped under the bed. A man I know is interned. . . . When I heard about it yesterday I couldn't stop crying.

'They might take my dad; they would come in the middle of the night. I often can't sleep for thinking about it and have to go into his room and see if he's still there. He hasn't done anything wrong, but neither had the others.

'The last time they came in they took some men away and as they were leaving they shouted "We'll be back for the rest tomorrow".'

Morris Fraser: *Children in Conflict*, 1973

Graph of deaths by violence in Northern Ireland, 1970–72

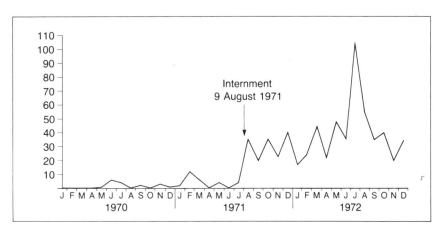

Internment also provoked a retaliatory campaign by the IRA. Faulkner never admitted, however, that internment was a mistake, and always rejected the figures that suggested that it increased the violence:

There are 'lies, damned lies and statistics'. The rate of increase of violence was in fact greater before internment than after. . . . How much violence would there have been without internment? . . .

I still believe that our security measures, of which internment was a very important point, were, by the end of 1971, beginning to pay off. . . .

Brian Faulkner: *Memoirs of a Statesman*, 1978

IRA retaliation to internment. On 5 October 1971 a bomb outside an army barracks kills a Scots Guard. Here, firemen, soldiers and police search through the wreckage for survivors

Questions

1 Do you believe Henry Bennett's statement? How would you check it?

2 What are the key features of British justice? How does internment measure up against them? Debate whether the government was right to remove certain human rights to try to defeat the IRA.

3 If internment did not stop IRA terrorism, why did the government continue to use it?

Further violence – Bloody Sunday

'As 1972 opened Northern Ireland presented a sorry picture to the world,' wrote Henry Kelly, an Irish journalist. The Catholics were angry at internment. The Protestants were despondent that it seemed to be failing. Unemployment and violence were both increasing. The English Secretary of State for Northern Ireland, Reginald Maudling, had even coined, in December 1971, the idea of an 'acceptable level of violence'.

Worse was to come. On Sunday 30 January 1972, the Civil Rights Association organised a march in Londonderry to protest against internment, despite a government ban. The local RUC chief wanted it to go ahead. The Army disagreed. They put up barriers to keep the march in the Bogside. In addition the tough First Battalion of the

Bloody Sunday. The Paras round up 'hooligans and rioters'

Parachute Regiment was ordered to conduct 'a scoop-up operation to arrest as many hooligans and rioters as possible'. Late in the afternoon, the Paras moved in. In the trouble that followed, 108 official rounds of ammunition were fired.

> The crowd flung themselves to the ground as the crack-crack of the self-loading rifles came from the bottom of Rossville Street. Looking up one could see the few stragglers coming running, panic-stricken, bounding over the barricade outside the High Flats, three of them stiffening suddenly and crumpling to the ground. One ought to have realised at the time that what was happening was that they were being killed. An hour and a half later no-one knew for certain how many were dead. Some said three, some five....
>
> The next morning there were groups of people standing around in Rossville Street, staring at the spots where it had happened. Everyone knew them now, the names of the dead. They could recite them as readily as a football fanatic rhymes off the names of his favourite team. And they knew how each one died, from the telling and retelling of it....
>
> After Bloody Sunday the most powerful feeling in the area was the desire for revenge....
>
> Eamonn McCann: *War and an Irish Town*, 1974

In fact, 13 people were killed on 'Bloody Sunday'. Major Hubert O'Neil, the Londonderry City Coroner, was in no doubt about who was to blame. At the inquest he said:

> It strikes me that the army ran amok that day and they shot without thinking of what they were doing. They were shooting innocent people. These people may have been taking part in a parade that

was banned — but I don't believe that justifies the firing of live rounds indiscriminately. I say it without reservation — it was sheer unadulterated murder.

Lord Widgery, the British Lord Chief Justice who chaired the official inquiry, was less hostile to the soldiers:

There would have been no deaths in Londonderry on 30 January if those who organised the illegal march had not thereby created a highly dangerous situation....

I am entirely satisfied that the first firing in the courtyard was directed at the soldiers.... There is no question of soldiers firing in panic to protect their own skins. They were too steady for that....

None of the deceased or wounded is proved to have been shot whilst handling a firearm or bomb. Some are wholly acquitted of complicity in such action; but there is a strong suspicion that some others had been firing weapons or handling bombs in the course of the afternoon and yet others had been closely supporting them.

HC 220: *Report of the Tribunal...*, 18 April 1972

acquitted: proved not guilty

And the soldiers themselves were more sceptical still:

They said we killed thirteen, wounded sixteen, all the rest of it. There is a distinct possibility that we took out more. All we could count were the bodies we could actually get to. We didn't assume anything: I'd have put the body count at thirty, not thirteen. I believe the extra bodies were whisked across the border.... Those bodies would have shown that the marchers had been infiltrated, manipulated. Instead, the IRA were able to turn it into a great propaganda exercise....

Sergeant, 1 Para, quoted in M. Arthur's book,
Northern Ireland Soldiers Talking, 1987

Whatever the truth of what happened that day, there was immediate reaction: a one-day strike, an illegal march of 50 000, a wave of IRA violence. A typical Catholic gravestone read: 'Sacred Heart of Jesus have mercy on the soul of HUGH PIUS GILMOUR, murdered by British Paratroopers on Bloody Sunday, 30th Jan. 1972, aged 17 years.'

Extreme Protestants, on the other hand, celebrated. One said on television that 'Loyalists called it "Good Sunday", and were only sorry that more IRA scum had not got what they clearly deserved'. The Protestant politician William Craig formed the new Vanguard Party, which demanded the extermination of the IRA and the repeal of all reforms.

On 24 March 1972 Edward Heath, the British Prime Minister, announced that Faulkner and his Cabinet had resigned, and that the Parliament at Stormont was suspended. The British government at Westminster had taken over 'Direct Rule' of Northern Ireland.

Questions

1. What facts can a historian learn from Eamonn McCann's account of Bloody Sunday?

2. Why did Hugh Gilmour die?

3. Why was there an 'explosion of Catholic anger' after Bloody Sunday?

4. Forensic reports revealed that:
   a) One of the dead men might have used a gun that afternoon.
   b) Nail bombs were found on one body (but not, surprisingly, at the first medical examination).
   c) In five cases, paraffin tests showed they had used a firearm, or had been close to someone who had used one.
   d) In three cases, there had been no contact with weapons.

   It is often said that the historian is a detective. Does this evidence prove that:
   i) Others had been firing weapons or handling bombs?
   ii) The troops were fired on?
   iii) The troops were fired on first?
   iv) The troops did not 'run amok and shoot without thinking'?

5. Compare Lord Widgery's comments after Bloody Sunday with those of the Cameron Commission after Burntollet (page 34). Are they similar in any way?

When the government uses force

At the height of the troubles, many Catholic areas had become 'no-go areas', where the police dared not go. The Catholic community kept its own law and order there. The Army broke the barricades down in July 1972 in Operation Motorman. The problem with such action

August 1972: the last barricade in the Bogside is dismantled. What was the photographer trying to show?

was that it drove moderates on both sides to support the extremists. The Oxford historian Charles Townshend believes that, since its job is to protect the citizens, the government was bound to use counter-force against the terrorists. Yet at the same time, he acknowledges, the government thereby appeared inhuman, created more opposition, and undermined its own position.

Questions

1 Draw up a list of suggestions which might, if followed, have stopped army action arousing opposition in the community.

2 Bernadette Devlin believes that 'if you hit [the Irish] they will hit back'. Do the events that occurred after Bloody Sunday prove that this is true? Are there any other events in modern Irish history which also prove that this statement is correct?

Using the evidence: the Army in Northern Ireland

Between 1971 and 1976 a total of 274 soldiers were killed in Northern Ireland. In July 1972 there were 21 300 troops on current operations. The following extracts will help you to form your own opinions about British Army operations in Ulster.

A On patrol with the Paras, 1973

Saracen: armoured vehicle used by the Army

We are meandering slowly back to Leopold Street via the back streets in low gear at high revs. The high-pitched whine of the Saracen in low gear is shattering, and guaranteed to wake even the heaviest of sleepers. Wake up you b......s! If we don't sleep, you don't. A couple of guys walking down the street with a girl. Great! Pile out of the Saracen, rifles levelled.

'Assume the position. Hands on the wall, fingers spread, now get those legs apart....'

boys: the people who would retaliate against anyone who co-operated with the Army

All our questions meeting no response. They're more afraid of what the 'boys' will do to them than what we have to offer. Soon change that, sunbeam. The dull thud of an idly swung baton.... Gasp of pain. [The soldiers conduct a physically painful body search of the men, and subject the girl to crude abuse.]

'O.K. lads, you've had your fun, back in the vehicle. Let's go.'

A.F.N. Clarke: *Contact*, 1983

B A great burden

Did I enjoy it? Well, yes and no. I enjoyed the comradeship. It's different there to what it is on any other tour of duty. Your

life depends on the chap behind you, and the chap in front of you, so you never fall out with each other – plus the bloke behind you has a loaded gun!

But the day I left, as I watched Belfast disappear into the distance and I knew I wouldn't be going back – it was like someone taking a great load off your shoulders. It was the worrying side of it that I didn't enjoy; I didn't enjoy the posting.

You've got to be alert all the time, and you've got to be tough. Christmas time, when you're cold and this woman comes out with a cup of coffee, it may have ground glass in the bottom; or a packet of chocolate might be drugged. This really happened whilst I was there. You can't relax, you can't be pleasant, because the longer you're stood still the greater the chance you'll be a sniper's target.

The worst people out there are the women. When you walk past they spit on you, and get the children to throw bottles at you because they know you can't attack the children. When you're attending a riot and you're in a snatch squad, they put the children at the front of the riot, and the adults stand at the back. At the back there'll be a sniper, too. One thing you have to look out for is when you go in, the crowd opens up, the sniper fires, and then the crowd closes in again to protect him. And if you're hit, they'll get you. You'd got to watch for that. And for the booby traps.

Heartbreak happens quite often – you get teased about what your girlfriend's up to back home, or you see a lad of six walking along the street carrying a loaded gun, or a grenade he'd found. It gets to you because they're just little children. They've been brought up to it: they've been permanently corrupted by it. It's upsetting.

I personally didn't lose any mates. But I did have to do a field dressing for a young soldier who'd had his eye put out by a bottle. They used to throw petrol bombs with rubber bands in them, so the burning rubber would stick to the skin; that was awful as well. One guy had his pub done over just because he'd served a Brit. You knew all those innocent people had been hurt just because of you. It was hard to handle. It was terrible knowing that if you bought a packet of cigarettes, you'd perhaps get the chap's shop burned down.

Private, Royal Pioneer Corps, on duty 1975–6,
talking to the author in 1988

C Modern riot gear makes the problem worse

The thicker the Army's protection gets...the more stoning goes on. When the Army had none of today's sophisticated

protection, soldiers... either ran away because they were hurt or went in, grabbed the child who had thrown the missile [and] took him back to his parents.... Now troops simply stand in line like statues.
    D. Barzilay: *The British Army in Ulster*, vol. 3, 1978

D   Not a job for a teenager

I think obviously the English people believe just what their sons believe when they come here – that they're here as a sort of peace-keeping force trying to keep the two warring religious factions apart.... The basic problem is just not as simple as that. If it was it maybe would have been cured long ago, but it goes much deeper than that, it's more complicated, and it certainly isn't a job for a young 18- or 19-year-old soldier to try to sort out.
    An anonymous Catholic on the ITV programme
    Too Long a Sacrifice, 1983

E

1   A.F.N. Clarke (source **A**) was a British officer. What is your reaction to his description of the behaviour of British troops?

2   Make a list of the different pressures placed upon British soldiers that are evident from source **B**.

3   Does it matter if the Army 'runs away' (source **C**)?

4   What are 'Force', 'Power', and 'Violence'? In what ways do the IRA and the British government use these 'weapons' differently? What makes the government's use of these 'weapons' more acceptable?

5   How might the two photographs in source **E** be used by the different sides in Northern Ireland? Does the camera ever lie?

5 THE CATHOLICS

Religion in society

In England today, religion is 'other-worldly'; it is concerned with things spiritual rather than practical. In Northern Ireland, religion is much more influential. Ulster people link it totally into their social lives, their jobs and their politics. In 1977 a survey in Limavady found that 84 per cent of Catholics (and 37 per cent of Protestants) went to church at least once a week. Religion is their attempt to understand the uncertainties of life: how people behave, setbacks and success, birth and death. Also, practically, the segregation of Catholics and Protestants adds a powerful reason to declare one's beliefs:

> *People are Protestants or Roman Catholics because...a person's religious beliefs...admit him to membership of a group of people which will provide him with the social support systems he needs in order to exist as a member of society. Within this group he finds his identity as a 'social' person; he knows who is like him and, equally important, who is not like him.*
> J. Hickey: *Religion and the Northern Ireland Problem*, 1984

A Catholic childhood

Gerry Adams was brought up in the Catholic Falls Road district of Belfast. His memories of childhood are typical. Being a Catholic is not just a matter of faith; Gerry Adams' whole personality was created by his environment. Even the children's songs of the 1950s encouraged Nationalist ideas:

> *When I was sick and very, very sick,*
> *And in my bed I lay,*
> *The only thing that cured my head*
> *Was to see the green flag fly.*

green flag: emblem of the Nationalist Party

And he was still a child when he first experienced sectarianism:

Mick: nickname for a Catholic

sally rod: rhyming slang for a 'Prod' – a Protestant

> *'Are you a Prod?' he challenged me. 'Are you a Prod or a Mick?' There were three of them, the biggest acting as interrogator while the other two blocked my exit....*
> *'Give him a hiding, Jimmy,' one of my assailant's smaller, runny-nosed confederates encouraged. 'He's a sally rod, give him the head, knock his melt in'....*
> *'Do you smoke?' asked snattery-nose. 'I'm dying for a fag.'*
> Gerry Adams: *Falls Memories*, 1982

Catholics growing up in the 1970s. What effect do you think these scenes will have had upon the children?

hurling/football/handball: traditional Gaelic sports

The Falls Road was a poor district, yet in spite of the deprivation Gerry Adams had a happy upbringing:

Summer evenings were spent in the Falls Park playing hurling and [Gaelic] football with infrequent formal handball sessions at the handball alley in St. Malachy's. During the winter we cadged money for the Clonard, Broadway or Diamond picture-houses or for the baths and, exams to one side, life was pleasant and uneventful.

Gerry Adams, as above

In his teens, Adams worked in a pub in the Protestant Shankill area of Belfast. He found the regulars kind, and almost sorry for him – 'If youse Fenians would just catch youselves on and stay quiet, everything would be okay.' But he grew to hate the disadvantages which

Catholics suffered: '...the lack of adult suffrage [voting rights], discrimination in jobs and housing, the gerrymandering of local government boundaries and the sectarian divisions.' Adams was already delivering election leaflets in the early 1960s. After the Paisley riots in 1966, he made the decision to leave school and go into politics:

We were all part of a new generation of working-class Taigs, winning scholarships to grammer [sic] schools and 'getting chances'.... By the end of 1964 I was merely an interested part of a small group which gathered in a dingy room in a Cyprus Street G.A.A. club to learn about Fenians and Fenianism, colonialism, neo-colonialism, partition and British imperialism. Sinn Fein, then an illegal organisation, was beginning to expand, and I was happy to be part of this new expansion.

Gerry Adams, as above

G.A.A.: Gaelic Athletic Association. The GAA has a controversial rule that members of the Crown forces cannot take part in Gaelic games

Fenians: Catholics (the names is taken from a nineteenth-century terrorist organisation)

Gerry Adams' name has been closely connected with the Provisional IRA. During the 1970s he rose to the leadership of Provisional Sinn Fein, the political party which supports the Provisional IRA.

Question

From this account of Gerry Adams' life, draw out the main beliefs and actions that characterise a 'Catholic'.

Gerry Adams arrives for a debate at the Oxford University Union in 1987

Using the evidence: Catholics speak for themselves

A We came very early to our politics. One learned, quite literally at one's mother's knee, that Christ died for the human race and Patrick Pearse for the Irish section of it. [We learned that many Irish martyrs] died in the fight to free Ireland from British rule, a fight which had paused in partial victory in 1922 when twenty-six of our thirty-two counties won their independence. It was our task to finish the job, to cleanse the remaining traces of foreign rule from the face of Ireland....
E. McCann: *War and an Irish Town*, 1974

Patrick Pearse: he led the 1916 Easter Rebellion. After his execution, he was regarded as a heroic martyr by the Irish Catholics

B The unemployment in our bones
Erupting in our hands in stones.
The thoughts of violence a relief,
The act of violence a grief.
Our bitterness and love,
Hand in glove.
Seamus Deane: *Derry*, 1974

C Tessie's lip curled... 'What change have we ever seen in the past 800 years? No change – nothing but poverty and injustice and humiliation. And who owns the Six Counties? We do! Not the people who are kicking us around. We own them. And we're going to get them back, no matter how many of us have to be tortured or killed or locked up for life. And when we have them back the others can stay if they behave themselves. We're not going to take it out on anyone once we have our rights. We've nothing against Prods or anyone else who calls himself an Irishman. But we're not going to stop fighting until we get our rights. And our rights are to rule over this country which we own. It doesn't belong to Britain and never has.'
Quoted in Dervla Murphy's book, *A Place Apart*, 1978

D   A Catholic view of the British Army

E   The Gaelic Athletic Association has two aims: to make traditional Gaelic games more popular, and to promote the Nationalist cause.

*The games are more than games – they have a national significance... to create a disciplined, self-reliant, national manhood which takes conscious pride in its heritage....
The native games... have been a part, and still are a part, of the nation's desire to live her own life, to govern her own affairs.... The national side of the G.A.A. and its dedication to the ideal of an Irish Ireland must be kept to the forefront at all times.*

Gaelic Athletic Association, *Rule Book*, 1970

1   Make a list of the feelings described in the above sources.

2   Identify events in Gerry Adams' childhood which might have contributed to the beliefs and opinions recorded in sources A–E.

Catholics and Northern Ireland

The sociologist John Hickey believes that the Catholics have their own way of looking at Northern Ireland. It involves a deep hostility towards Britain.

[They have built up a picture] of an Irish nation subjugated and divided by many centuries of conquest and unable to fulfil its own

destiny because of...the English who attempted to impose an alien rule and culture.

John Hickey: *Religion and the Northern Ireland Problem*, 1984

Yet, as we have seen, most Catholics living in Northern Ireland do not want unity with Eire. The Limavady survey found that only 14 per cent of Catholics wanted to become part of Eire – as many as wanted Direct Rule by Britain! – while 50 per cent preferred some kind of power sharing (see Chapter 6) with the Protestants.

Also, psychologists studying the attitudes of northern Catholics have found that they do not generally have the underlying psychological fears or hatreds to be found amongst Protestants. In 1977, the psychologist E.E. O'Donnell analysed Catholic feelings about Protestants. He found that the description they used most was 'power-holders'. After that, in order of frequency of usage, came: 'bigoted', 'Loyalist', 'British', 'bitter', 'ordinary people', 'brainwashed' and 'determined'. 'Murderers' came last of all, and was used mainly among Belfast working-class women. Catholics, Hickey concluded, do not hate Protestants; they just hate what Protestants do. We find this in other sources. According to Bernadette Devlin:

[My teacher] didn't hate Protestants, but her view was that you couldn't very well put up with them, they weren't Irish....

B. Devlin: *Price of My Soul*, 1969

And Eamonn McCann remembers:

We were never taught to hate Protestants. Rather we were taught to accept that it was for the best that we did not know them. [When taunted,] we told one another to 'just ignore them'.

E. McCann: *War and an Irish Town*, 1974

IRA council. From left to right: Martin McGuinness, alleged commander Derry IRA; David O'Connell, thought to have smuggled arms; Sean MacStiofan, IRA Chief of Staff; Seamus Twomey, Belfast brigade commander

---

Coursework assignment: the Provos

Skill: looking at history from the perspective of people in the past

A *Copy of the IRA political and military plan, received by RUC mid-1968 from A.1 source*

Stages: 1. Anti-agent campaign (start immediately).
2. Large stunt-type operations.
3. Escalation.
4. Final phase (agricultural and industrial sabotage to take place at this stage).
5. Opportunity to kidnap prominent British government members should be availed of when it arises. (Publicity)....

Retaliatory action to be taken against selected (agent-type) RUC men. Military action against the British Army should also be considered.

Equipment: 10 ton plastic explosives. Timing devices. 5,000 grenades, 1,000 shortarms (9mm or .45 automatic). 1,000,000 rounds of revolver ammo. 200 automatic rifles (F.N.) 100,000 rounds of rifle ammo. 300 bazookas and 3,000 shells.

Command Paper 566: *Violence and Civil Disturbances in 1969* (The Scarman Tribunal), vol. 2, Appendix B, 1972

Declaration of 1916: the Declaration of Irish Independence which started the 1916 rebellion

The British are imperialist and colonialist exploiters: they want to build an Empire purely for England's benefit

B *We are not interested in seeking public support of any kind for our actions: we are convinced that the Declaration of 1916 gives us the right and the duty to eject the British from Ireland by whatever means we choose....*

No British Government proposals can ever be trusted.... The British are imperialist and colonialist exploiters; they are implacably hostile to Ireland and they must be driven out....

A Provo speaking in 1972, quoted in T.E. Utley's book, *Lessons of Ulster*, 1975

C *'Provo thinking' is a misleading phrase. The Provos don't think; they inherit fixed attitudes and on the basis of those they feel deeply and act ruthlessly...they believe themselves to be wearing the armour of righteousness....*

[They have] very high standards of discipline and very firm principles about what is allowable under war conditions. If the wrong person is killed...that is considered a tragedy and the Provos mean it when they say they are sorry. But such occasional accidents are seen as inevitable, however regrettable.

To them their campaign is, in a curious way, a conventional war, and they want to keep the party clean. The fact that most people regard them as an especially dirty

IRA in training

bunch of urban guerilla terrorists they find incomprehensible and very wounding.

Dervla Murphy: *A Place Apart*, 1978

D   We don't defend the killing of innocent people at all: the IRA doesn't even defend innocent people being killed. The fact of the matter is that we are strongly convinced that the responsibility for every death in Ireland, whether it be the death of a British soldier, an IRA man, an RUC man, a UDR man, or innocent civilians – at the end of the day responsibility for all that lies at the feet of the British Government. They are the people responsible because they partitioned this country against the overwhelming wishes of the Irish people. They are the people who must pick up the tab.

Martin McGuinness, Sinn Fein candidate, talking on the BBC programme *Real Lives*, 1985

E   Gerry Adams and young supporters

1. Many people, including the British Prime Minister, Margaret Thatcher, think of terrorists as 'men of blood', 'nasty urban guerillas', 'psychopaths'. The psychologist, H. Cleckley, in his book *The Mask of Sanity* (1964), outlined the following characteristics of psychopaths:

   charming and intelligent;
   unreliable, untruthful and insincere;
   lack of guilt or shame;
   cannot give, or accept, love or friendship;
   failure to follow any life plan;
   thoughtless antisocial behaviour.

   Before writing the assignment essay, discuss whether or not the Provos, as described in the above sources, are 'psychopaths'. Why are they able to kill without mercy?

2. Write an essay describing the thoughts and feelings that would have led an IRA Provisional to plant a bomb in a public place in the 1970s. Write in the third person – 'He would have felt. . . .' Remember that you cannot be certain of his feelings, so use words like 'perhaps' and 'possibly'. Wherever possible, support your ideas with quotes from the sources. Note that you are being asked to 'empathise' with this man, not to sympathise with him.

IRA bomb near Scotland Yard

6 IN SEARCH OF AN ANSWER

Power sharing, 1974

Direct Rule was followed by one of the most confused and dangerous periods in the history of Northern Ireland, during which the Secretary of State, William Whitelaw, tried to find a political solution. In September 1972 Whitelaw talked with Ulster politicians in Darlington, County Durham, about the future of Northern Ireland. Afterwards, the British government issued a White Paper (March 1973) proposing an Ulster 'Assembly' elected by proportional representation. The Assembly, it was planned, would look after all Northern Ireland's internal affairs except security.

The White Paper included two new ideas. Firstly, it proposed a Council of Ireland where southern and northern politicians would meet to discuss Ulster's affairs. Secondly, it suggested the idea of 'power sharing': the new government would have to include Catholic as well as Protestant ministers. The government's aim was to unite reasonable men from both sides. It hoped that many Ulster people would join the Alliance Party, a non-sectarian party formed in 1970.

For a while, the plan seemed to be succeeding. Faulkner and the Official Unionists agreed to take part. The SDLP – the moderate Catholic party – also declared its support.

William Whitelaw

Leaders of the moderate Catholic SDLP. Left, John Hume; right, Gerry Fitt

State of the parties in the power-sharing Assembly, June 1973

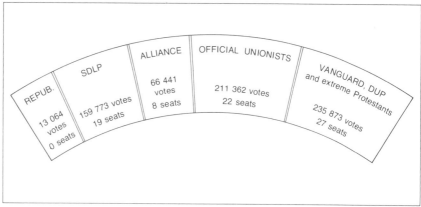

The elections on 28 June 1973 gave a majority to the Faulknerite–SDLP–Alliance coalition. On the basis of this, the government pressed ahead. In December 1973, at Sunningdale in Berkshire, a Britain–Eire–Ulster conference created the Council of Ireland. On 1 January 1974, the new ministers took office. The membership list of the Executive of chief ministers shows the idea of power sharing:

Chief Executive	Brian Faulkner	(Unionist)
Deputy	Gerry Fitt	(SDLP)
Finance	Herbert Kirk	(Unionist)
Commerce	John Hume	(SDLP)
Education	Basil McIvor	(Unionist)
Housing	Austin Currie	(SDLP)
Environment	Roy Bradford	(Unionist)
Law Reform	Oliver Napier	(Alliance)

In the meantime, however, the extreme Protestants had been growing angry. Protestant workers united in the Loyalist Association of Workers (LAW) led by Billy Hull, a right-wing union boss. A Loyalist paramilitary group was created called the Ulster Defence Association (UDA). Their mood is shown in a letter to the UDA newspaper in February 1972, criticising the Protestant leaders:

Why have they not started to hit back in the only way these nationalist b......s understand? That is ruthless indiscriminate killing.... If I had a flame-thrower I would roast the slimy excreta that pass for human beings.

There was a string of horrific sectarian killings. On 13 August 1972 Thomas Madden, a Catholic, was kidnapped. His captors hung him up by his arms and stabbed him 150 times before eventually strangling him.

In May 1974 all the extreme Protestant groups united and set up the Ulster Workers Council (UWC). They called a general strike to destroy the power-sharing Executive.

Meanwhile, IRA terrorism continued. In February 1974, 12 soldiers and civilians were killed when a coach was blown up on the M62 in England. Violence became a powerful weapon in Ulster politics, driving people on both sides to extreme positions. Moderate politicians who 'kept their heads' lost votes. Faulkner's position crumbled. Soon after taking office as Chief Executive he lost his position as Unionist leader.

The UWC strike (14–28 May 1974) was the last straw which destroyed the Executive. Many observers believe it took Ulster to the brink of anarchy (complete lawlessness). Power cuts brought industry to a halt and threatened the pumping stations which alone prevented large areas of Belfast from being flooded with raw sewage. Doctors, social workers and bakers queued to get 'essential petrol' tickets from UDA terrorists. Executive ministers and advisers were intimidated. After the strike a right-wing Army Lieutenant boasted that even the Army had refused to break the strike:

The Army decided that it was right and that it knew best and the politicians had better toe the line.

Monday World, Summer 1974

On the morning of 28 May 1974, Faulkner went to see Merlyn Rees (Secretary of State from March 1974). He told him that he was going to resign to prevent the possibility of suffering and loss of life – 'The degree of consent needed to sustain the Executive does not at present exist.' Protestants celebrated. The power-sharing experiment had collapsed.

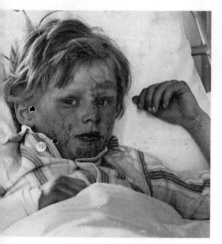

Bernard Lynch, an eight-year-old Catholic, recovers in hospital after a gang of Protestant youths poured petrol over him, then set him alight. What impact do you think this photograph would have had on the Catholic community?

The 1974 strike: extreme Loyalist Protestants bring down the power-sharing Executive

Merlyn Rees (right) and Brian Faulkner in happier times

Questions

1 What activities would grind to a halt without electricity?

2 What do you think was the key factor in the failure of the power-sharing experiment?

3 William Whitelaw held talks with the IRA leaders in July 1972. He has been greatly criticised for this. Is it a good or bad idea to negotiate with terrorists?

Using the evidence: atrocity, 1978

Ulster Protestants believe that people in England do not fully understand what it is like to live under the threat of the IRA, or the true horror of an IRA atrocity. After the La Mon Restaurant bombing described below, James Kilfedder, Unionist MP for Down North, told the House of Commons:

> *Innocent people in the Province are daily and hourly at risk and facing death, such as the tearing apart and burning alive that occurred in the Lamon House Restaurant explosion. I was shown a piece of skull with hair attached to it, one of the remnants of the human remains that were found in the debris of the explosion. That is an example of what should be shown to people throughout the country to make them aware of how the Ulster people are suffering.*
>
> Hansard, 20 February 1978

Yet the La Mon explosion was only one of many IRA attacks. People in England gain information about such events second-hand, through newspapers such as *The Times*. The following extracts will allow you to consider just how adequately they are reported.

A *14 die in bomb attack on packed Ulster restaurant*

> *At least 14 people were killed and 21 seriously injured last night in one of the worst terrorist attacks in Northern Ireland since the present troubles began in 1969. The bombs exploded at La Mon House, a complex of bars and restaurants in Co. Down, 14 miles from Belfast. About four hundred and fifty people were in the roadhouse.... As members of the emergency services struggled through the smoking ruins early today it became obvious that some of the victims were children who had been attending one of the two main functions being held in the restaurant at the time of the attack.*
>
> *One witness said: 'I have never experienced such a ghastly sight in all my life. Small charred bundles of what had*

been people were being dragged out and there seemed no way of knowing how many were still inside.'

The Northern Ireland Junior Motor Cycle Club was one of the organizations holding a function in the restaurant.

The Times, Saturday 18 February 1978

B   Until late last night the process of formally identifying the charred remains of the 12 dead continued, with the use of dental records and hair samples from their homes. The results confirmed that most of the victims were Protestants.

Ten of the 12 dead were members of the Irish Collie Club, which was holding its annual dinner when the bombers struck, attaching their lethal device outside the restaurant with a hook. The explosion blew burning petrol across the room....

The Times, Monday 20 February 1978

On Monday *The Times* also printed the statements about the bombing made by the IRA and the RUC:

C   The IRA admits responsibility for the bombing operation at La Mon House in which 12 innocent people died. There is nothing we can offer in mitigation bar that our enquiries have established that a nine-minute warning was given to the RUC. This proved totally inadequate, given the disastrous consequences.

We accept condemnation and criticism from only two sources: from the relatives and friends of those who were accidentally killed and from our supporters who have rightly and severely criticised us.... All killings and tragedies stem from British interference and the denial of Irish sovereignty. The IRA will continue to resist the British with all the might that we can muster.

IRA statement, quoted verbatim in *The Times*, Monday 20 February 1978

D   A call was made to a telephone operator at 8.57 p.m., warning that a bomb was in the restaurant. At exactly the same time the bomb exploded. When the operator rang us, we immediately dispatched a patrol to the scene and then telephoned the hotel. A man answered at the other end and without asking who was on the telephone said: 'A bomb has gone off' and slammed the phone down. There was no warning at all and the words of the Provisional IRA will not bring back the 12 people who died.

RUC statement, quoted verbatim in *The Times*, Monday 20 February 1978

The Times also reported the reactions of various people. The SDLP leader Gerry Fitt called the IRA 'savage animals', and the Sinn Fein president called them the 'mad Provos'. Others commented:

E *If those who contribute [to IRA funds] believe their money goes to support widows and orphans, let me make it clear that it goes to make widows and orphans.*
J. Lynch, Eire Prime Minister, quoted in *The Times*, Monday 20 February 1978

F *I have never been under such strong pressure from the grass-roots to authorize some kind of immediate action. But at this stage, my advice to all on the loyalist side is to exercise restraint. It would be totally wrong for this terrible attack to be immediately overtaken by violent reaction; the full effect must be allowed to sink in on everyone.*
Andy Tyrie, UDA leader, quoted in *The Times*, Monday 20 February 1978

G *We feel helpless in a society in which law appears to protect the criminal, and attitudes inevitably harden. We must make increasing demands for changes in the law which will ensure that criminals are brought to justice and the proper punishment to fit their horrible crimes.*
Rev. W.J. McKinstry Wallace at the funeral of bomb victims Ian and Elizabeth McCraken, quoted in *The Times*, Wednesday 22 February 1978

1 List the facts in the extracts which shock you. Do you think that *The Times* fully conveys the horror of the bombing?

2 Do you believe the IRA (source C) or the RUC (source D) about whether or not a nine-minute warning was given? Justify your choice.

3 How did the IRA explain the event? Discuss your feelings about their explanation.

4 Describe and document the range of different Protestant reactions to the atrocity.

5 Consider the following alternatives. A bombing such as the La Mon Restaurant explosion:
a) explains the violence of some Protestants;
b) excuses the violence of some Protestants;
c) justifies the violence of some Protestants.
Which do you think is the most correct statement? Discuss your answer in class.

The hunger strike

After the failure of power sharing, a British politician admitted: 'Merlyn [Rees] and I hadn't a clue where we were going.' The British Cabinet even discussed such 'radical constitutional initiatives' as complete British withdrawal, and repartition.

Meanwhile, however, the IRA was re-organising under the influence of Gerry Adams. It admitted that it could never 'drive the British into the sea', and sought to develop Provisional Sinn Fein (PSF) as a political party. The approach, said Adams, must be both 'the ballot box and the bomb'. Terrorism was reduced. The PSF leaders looked for an opportunity to win more general Catholic support. It was provided by the IRA prisoners in the Maze prison who were demanding that they be treated as political prisoners. They wanted concessions on work, visits and clothes. Some of them began a 'Dirty Protest' (sometimes called the 'Blanket Protest'). They refused to wash, daubed excrement on their cell walls, and wore only a blanket. In March 1981 Bobby Sands, the Provos' commanding officer in the Maze, began a hunger strike. Other Provos followed his example. Margaret Thatcher, the British Prime Minister, let it be known that she would not give way to the terrorists' demands.

The sight of IRA hunger-strikers starving themselves to death won the PSF massive Catholic support. Observers noticed how it seemed to appeal directly to their 'tribal voice of martyrdom'. Richard Ford, a reporter on *The Times*, summed up the results of the British government's stand:

Headquarters of the H-block strike committee. Why are there boulders outside?

INLA: another extreme Nationalist terrorist group

H-block: the barracks in the Maze are built in the shape of and 'H'

Dail: the Eire Parliament

In the 216 days since Bobby Sands started the hunger strike on March 1... ten republican prisoners, members of the IRA or Irish National Liberation Army, starved themselves to death.... Seventy-five civilians and members of the security forces have died this year compared with 76 for all of 1980....

Thousands attended the funerals of the hunger strikers. Recruits flocked to join [the IRA]. Its coffers were swelled with collections in the United States....

The Prince of Wales on a visit to New York earlier this year was greeted by anti H-block demonstrators and the Government later advised Princess Margaret to cancel a trip to the United States....

Before his death, Sands had been elected MP for Fermanagh, South Tyrone.... In the Irish Republic one hunger striker and a republican prisoner were elected to the Dail.... the name of Bobby Sands, aged 27, a member of the IRA from Belfast and serving 14 years for possession of a gun, brought demonstrations to the streets of New York, Paris and Rome. In Tehran [the capital of Iran] a street was named after him.

The Times, 5 October 1981

Coursework assignment: the hunger strike

Skill: putting modern events into historical context

Emotional departures

The death of hunger-striker Patsy O'Hara naturally taxed the emotions of the O'Hara family who had been under eight weeks of distress and suffering, closely monitoring his condition and offering him their support.

Patsy's brother on the blanket, Tony, ... states: 'I saw Patsy for half-an-hour on Thursday morning and for three-quarters of an hour on Thursday night before being taken back to my cell. He was in a coma at this stage.

'The last time I was actually speaking to him was on Monday and he was very disoriented. He was dubious about the things that he was thinking. He said that he had some sort of dreams that were way out. ...

'We had been talking about the old times, when we were kids, about the house, what we were going to do when we got out and so on. He had been in good form.

'But we did not show our feelings to the screws, because Patsy would not have wanted that, for me to break down crying in front of the screws. So I just held back as best I could.

'He died fighting for his country and his fellow comrades. He served them.'

SEAN SEAMUS
Another brother, Sean Seamus, says that when the family were urgently summoned to the hospital on the Wednesday evening, the day before Patsy died, just shortly after he took a heart attack, they were delayed at the prison gate for over half-an-hour before being eventually allowed in. ...

ELIZABETH
When Patsy died at half-past eleven that night, his father, twenty-one-year-old sister Elizabeth, family friend James Daly, two priests, two prison warders, and a doctor, were present. ...
[Elizabeth] recalls the agony of that evening:

'A priest had been sitting with Patsy and he came out and told us he was dead. That was at about ten o'clock or half-past ten. When we went into the room he was still alive. They thought he was dead because his heart had stopped and he tried to breathe but he breathed very hard after that.

'And his face was full of pain. About twenty past eleven then he gave his last breath. ... And as he was dying his face just changed, he had a very, very distinct smile on his face which I will never forget. I said, "You're free Patsy. You have won your fight. And you're free." And he was cold then.'

Republican News, 30 May 1981

Bobby Sands' funeral cortege, 5 July 1981

1. What facts about the hunger strike can a historian learn from the article 'Emotional departures'?

2. Why did Patsy O'Hara die?

3. Select an event or sequence of events from Ireland's history which you think is similar to the events of the hunger strike. Explain the similarities.

4. Why did the hunger strike have such a great effect on the Catholics of Northern Ireland?

Prior's policy

By September 1981 the British government had realised the need for new ideas. Mrs Thatcher appointed James Prior, a leading Tory moderate, as Secretary of State for Northern Ireland.

1981

14 Sept. James Prior becomes Northern Ireland Secretary. He has talks with all the different groups, including the IRA prisoners in the Maze.

5 Oct. The hunger strike ends. Prior immediately gives concessions to the prisoners on work, visits and clothes.

10 Oct. IRA nail bomb at Chelsea Barracks in London kills two people. An IRA statement claims the reason for the bomb is 'the state of war which exists between the British government who occupy Ireland, and the oppressed Irish people who strike out through the IRA'.

26 Oct. IRA bomb in London's Oxford Street kills the expert trying to defuse it.

James Prior looking tired

7 Nov.	A White Paper proposes an 'Anglo-Irish Intergovernmental Council'. Paisley promises to destroy 'this fresh attempt to hand us over to the enemy'.
14 Nov.	Unionist MP the Rev. Bradford killed by the IRA.
16 Nov.	Paisley expelled from the House of Commons after protesting there. Prior says: 'The more reaction, the more we are playing into the hands of the IRA,' but promises to improve security.
19 Nov.	Sixteen anti-terrorist squads and Spearhead battalions sent to Ulster. Loyalists form vigilante groups. Prior says: 'Private armies have no place in society.'
23 Nov.	Paisley organises a Day of Action – a general strike and a march of 10 000 men whom he calls the Third Force.

vigilante groups: people who take the law into their own hands

1982

6 Jan.	Economic aid for N. Ireland increased to £3150 million, estimated to result in 12 500 new jobs and 4500 new houses.
6 April	A White Paper proposes a Northern Ireland Assembly. It includes the idea of 'Rolling Devolution' – Ulster politicians gradually taking over more of their own government as they feel able. It hopes Catholics and Protestants 'may achieve sufficient mutual respect...to live together as good neighbours'.
13 July	It is the 'Year of the Supergrass'. The government has made hundreds of arrests based on the evidence of informers. The IRA kidnap Fiona Brown, the wife of an informer.

20 July	Bombs in Hyde Park and Regent's Park in London.
Sept.	IRA bombing campaign.
20 Oct.	Elections for the Assembly give extremist groups many seats (DUP, 20; OUP, 24; SDLP, 13; PSF, 5). The *Daily Express* calls the election 'Prior's bloody shambles'. Prior is called 'the man who put the IRA into a Northern Ireland Assembly'.

Questions

1. Demonstrate from the events of 1981–2 the policies of the British government in Northern Ireland as regards:
   a) the political situation;
   b) the security situation;
   c) the economic situation.

2. Describe and explain the reactions of both the IRA and the extreme Protestants to the British government's policies.

3. Monitor a current IRA atrocity and the reactions to it. Compare the sequence of events with those of 1981–2.

"The only solution to the Irish problem is to understand that no solution works"

Appendix I

Southern Ireland (or 'Eire', or 'the Twenty-Six Counties') is an independent country, and is Catholic. Its capital is *Dublin*.

Northern Ireland (or 'Ulster' or 'the Six Counties') is part of the United Kingdom, although from 1921 to 1972 it had its own parliament at *Stormont*. The main cities are *Londonderry* and *Belfast*.

Catholics/Nationalists

The Catholics are the *minority* in Northern Ireland. *Nationalists* want independence from England. They want to become part of Eire (Southern Ireland). The political party *Sinn Fein* won independence for Southern Ireland in 1921. Sinn Fein leaders today include *Gerry Adams* and *Martin McGuinness*. Many Catholics are *Republican*: they do not want (the British) monarchy. The *Irish Republican Army* (IRA) is the military wing of Sinn Fein. Since 1969 a breakaway group, the *Provisional IRA* ('Provos'), has been responsible for most of the terrorism in Northern Ireland. IRA Provos such as *Bobby Sands* starved themselves to death in the hunger strikes of 1981. Much of the money which supports these groups comes from Irish Americans through an organisation called *NORAID*.

Few Catholics support terrorism. In the 1960s the *Northern Ireland Civil Rights Association* (NICRA) went on marches to try to get housing and local government reforms. NICRA leaders included *Bernadette Devlin*, *Eamonn McCann* and *Michael Farrell*.

In 1970 the *Social and Democratic Labour Party* (SDLP) was formed. It wants to obtain a united Ireland by peaceful, political means. The SDLP has been prepared to co-operate with the British government. *John Hume* and *Gerry Fitt* are prominent SDLP supporters.

Catholics are nicknamed '*Micks*' and '*Taigs*' by Protestants, or *Fenians* (after a nineteenth-century terrorist organisation), or '*Papists*' (after the Pope). The *Gaelic Athletic Association* (GAA) aims to spread the popularity of the traditional Irish games, culture and language.

Protestants/Unionists

Protestants ('*Prods*') are the *majority* in Northern Ireland. Unionists (or '*Loyalists*') want Ulster to remain Protestant, and part of the United Kingdom. The most prominent early Unionist was *Sir Edward Carson*. The *Official Unionist Party* (OUP) held power from the 1920s until 1972. Prime Ministers have been *Sir James Craig* (1921-40), *Lord Brookeborough* (1943-63), *Captain Terence O'Neill* (1963-69), *Sir James Chichester-Clark* (1969-71), *Brian Faulkner* (1971-2). *The B-Specials* (armed, Protestant, special police disbanded in 1970) supported the Unionist Party.

Extreme Protestant groups have included *Vanguard* (from 1972); the *Loyalist Association of Workers* ('LAW': 1972); the *Ulster Workers Council* (UWC: 1974). The *Democratic Unionist Party* (DUP) was formed in 1971 by *Ian Paisley*.

Many Protestants are in the *Orange Order*, sworn to defend the union with England and the Protestant faith. Protestant terrorist groups include the *Ulster Volunteer Force* (UVF), the *Ulster Defence Association* (UDA) and the *Ulster Freedom Fighters* (UFF).

The British government has ruled Ulster directly from Westminster ('*Direct Rule*') since 1972 through a *Secretary of State* – for example *William Whitelaw*, *Merlyn Rees* and *James Prior*.

The government is supported by the *Regular Army*, units such as the *SAS*, and also by the police (the *Royal Ulster Constabulary* – RUC) and by a part-time regiment, the *Ulster Defence Regiment* (UDR). Although both Catholics and Protestants are encouraged to join the RUC and the UDR, the RUC is 90 per cent Protestant, and the UDR is 97 per cent Protestant.

Appendix II

A *The violence in Belfast reached its climax in May and June. There was constant heavy firing into the Catholic ghettoes and Catholics were killed at random. The IRA didn't take direct sectarian reprisals though some Catholic defence groups did. But their efforts were puny compared with the Specials and the armed Loyalist groups, who operated murder squads designed to take immediate reprisals for all IRA action and generally to terrorise the Catholic population into a state of abject submission....*
     M. Farrell: *Northern Ireland: The Orange State*, 1976

B *The second and third weeks were particularly bad. The IRA certainly seems to have set the pace, not always confining their activities to 'empty warehouses and uninhabited castles....' Belfast was the main centre of disturbance. On the weekend of 22 May fourteen deaths occurred, deaths described by the* Northern Whig *as callous, deliberate murders, and in the following week there were twenty-two outbreaks of fire, directed chiefly against Protestant business premises in the Catholic districts.*
     P. Buckland: *Ulster Unionism... 1886–1922*, 1973

Appendix III

A was written by an Ulster Protestant. Note that he expects Catholics also to admire Paisley – Protestant 'elitism'? (*Belfast Telegraph*, 30 August 1972.)

B was written by an Englishwoman. Many English people find Ulster Protestantism unreasonable and unpleasant. Why? (*Today*, 23 July 1986.)

C was written by a Catholic from Southern Ireland. (Dervla Murphy: *A Place Apart*, 1978.)

D was said by an IRA Catholic. Many Provisionals are socialist, and see Protestant extremists as their working-class equals. (Quoted in Dervla Murphy's book, as above.)

Skills grid

Key
U Using the evidence
Q Questions
C Coursework assignment

A Historical skills

1 *Using historical evidence*

	U	U	Q	U	U	Q	U	U	Q	U	U	Q	Q	Q	Q	U	U	Q	U	C	Q	U	C	Q
	7	10	13	16	18	21	24	25	29	35	40	43	44	49	50	52	60	64	67					
Comprehension of variety of sources	■	■																						
Extraction of information											■	■												
Evaluation, recognising * fact *v* opinion					■																			
* bias							■				■													
* importance of origin and context																								
Recognition of inference and implication in a source		■			■																			
Comparison of different sources based on relative reliability													■				■							
Reaching conclusions on basis of this comparison													■											
Recognising gaps and inconsistencies		■																						
Judgement and choice between various opinions																								
Formation of overview and synthesis of one's own opinion																								

2 *Empathy*

| Understanding events and issues from perspective of people in the past | | | | | | | | | | | | | | | | | | | | | | | | |

B Historical concepts

Cause and consequence	■											■												
Continuity and change												■												
Similarity and difference																								
Interaction of individual with society			■																					
Historical vocabulary and terminology														■										

INDEX

Numerals in **bold** denote illustrations

Adams, Gerry, 47–9, **49**, 54, 63, 68
Alliance Party, 56, 57
Anglo-Irish Council, 56–7
Army, 6, 35, 36, 38, 39, 40–42, **41**, 43, **43**, 44–6, **46**, **51**, 53, 54, 58, 63, 66, 69, **70**

barricades, 35, 43, **43**
Belfast, 7, 9, 10, 11, 12, 22, **23**, **26**, 32, 36, 45, 48, 52, 58, 63, 68, 69
Bloody Sunday (10.7.21), 7
Bloody Sunday (30.1.72), 40, **41**, 42
Brookeborough, Lord Basil, 12, 28, 68
Burntollet, 32–4, **33**

Callaghan, James, 35
Cameron Commission (1969), 14, 30, 34
Campaign for Social Justice, 37
Carson, Sir Edward, 6, **6**, 25, 68
Chichester-Clark, James, 36, 68
childhood, **10**, 39, 47–8, **48**, 50, 52, **70**
Civil Rights, *see* NICRA
Clones incident, 10
Covenant, Solemn League and, 6, 25
Craig, Sir James, 6, 8, 13, 30, 68
Craig, William, 42

Dail Eireann, 5, 6, 63
Derry Citizens Defence Assoc., 35
Devlin, Bernadette, 30, **30**, **31**, 32, 44, 52, 68
Direct Rule, 42, 56, 69
Dirty Protest, 63
discrimination, 16–17, 29, 30
DUP, 21, 26, 57, 67, 69

Easter Rebellion, 5, 50, 53
economy, 11–12, 15, **15**, 16–17, 29, 30, 50, 58, 66
Eire (Free State), 5, 6, 8, 10, 11, 19, 28, 29, 36, 52, 57, 62, 63, 68
European Court of Human Rights (Strasbourg), 19, 38

Farrell, Michael, 33, 68
Faulkner, Brian, 30, 36–9, 42, 56, 57, 58, **59**, 68
Fitt, Gerry, 57, 62, 68

Gaelic Athletic Assoc., 49, 51, 68
gerrymandering, 13–16, 30, 49

Haughey, Charles, 36
Heath, Edward, 36, 42
housing, 14, 15, **16**, **23**, **24**, **26**, 29, 66
Hume, John, 57, 68
hunger strike, 63–5, **64**, **65**

industrial sabotage, 9, 11, 36, 69
INLA, 63
internment, 8, 11, 36–40, **37**
IRA, 5, 6, 7, 8, 9, 10, 11, 19, 21, 24, 26, 28, 31, 32, 36, 38, 39, **40**, 42, 68, 69 (*see also* Provos)

LAW, 58, 69
La Mon Restaurant, 60–62
Londonderry, 6, 13–16, **13**, **15**, **16**, **24**, 30, 31–2, 34–5, **34**, 40–42, 68

Maudling, Reginald, 40
Maze prison, 63, 65
McCann, Eamonn, 15, 30, 32–3, 41, 52, 68
McGuinness, Martin, **52**, 68
Motorman Operation, 43

Nationalist Party, 5, 13, 14, 16, 28, 47, 51, 52, 57, 68
NICRA, 30–32, **31**, 40, 68
NILP, 12, 30
no-go areas, 43
NORAID, 63, 68

O'Hara, Patsy, 64–5, **64**
O'Neil, Major Hubert, 41
O'Neill, Captain Terence, 22, 28–30, **29**, 32–3, 35, 68
Orange Order, 9, 11, 18, **18**, 23, 24, **25**, 29, 36, 69
Orange, William of, 25

Paisley, Rev. Ian, 20–22, **20**, 66, 69

Partition Treaty (6.12.21), 5, 8
People's Democracy, 30, 32–4
pogrom, 6, 8
power sharing, 56–9
Prior, James, 65, **66**, 67, **67**, 69
proportional representation, 14, 56
Provos, 36, 49, 52–5, **52**, **54**, **55**, 58, 60–62, 63, 65–7, 68 (*see also* IRA)
PSF, 49, 63, 67

Rees, Merlyn, 58, **59**, 63, 69
refugees, **10**
RUC, 9, 14, 31–4, 40, 53, 54, 61, 69

Sands, Bobby, 63, **65**, 68
SDLP, 56, 57, 67, 68
sectarian incidents, 7, 9, 12, 20, 24, 35, 47, 58, **58**, 69
Sinn Fein, 5, 6, 8, 11, 12, 49, 68
Special Powers Act, 8, 38
Specials, 7, 9, 10, 11, 22, 30, 33, 35, 68, 69
Spence, Gusty, 25, 29
Stormont, 8, 13, 14, 29, 42, 68
strike (1974), 58–9, **59**
Sunningdale, 57
Supergrass, 66
Swanzy, D.P.I., 6, 7

Thatcher, Margaret, 55, 63, 65, **67**

UDA, 24, **27**, 58, 62, 69
UDR, 69
UFF, 69
Ulster Assembly, 56, 57, **57**, 66, 67
Ulster Protestant Assoc., 7
Unionist Party, 5, 6, 11, 12, 13, 14, 15, 28, 29, 56, **57**, 60, 66, 67, 68
UVF, 69
UWC, 58, 69

Valera, Eamonn de, **5**, 11
Vanguard Party, 42, 69

Whitelaw, William, 56, **56**, 69
White Paper (1973), 56
White Paper (1982), 66
Widgery Report, 42, 43
Wilson, Harold, 28, 35